LORI LYTLE
illustrated by **LEO SCOPACASA**

The Unifying
CONSCIOUSNESS
TAROT

*May you be guided by
the Unifying Consciousness of Love.*

❖ ❖ ❖

*Deepest thanks to Matthew
and Joseph for your love, support, and faith in
us throughout this adventure.*

◆ ◆ ◆

CONTENTS

MEET
The Unifying Consciousness Tarot | 9

♦ ♦ ♦

THE ANATOMY OF
The Unifying Consciousness Tarot | 17

♦ ♦ ♦

MAJOR ARCANA | 23

♦ ♦ ♦

MINOR ARCANA | 74

♦ ♦ ♦

The Suits and Their Elements | 76

The Numbers | 82

Court Cards | 85

How to Use the Activation | 87

Wands | 88

Cups | 104

Swords | 121

Pentacles | 138

♦ ♦ ♦

How to Read Tarot | 157

Setting the Scene | 158

Invocation | 159

Forming the Question | 160

Choosing a Tarot Spread | 160

Shuffling the Cards | 161

Laying Out and Reading the Cards | 161

Closing the Reading | 163

Tarot Spreads | 164

About the Creators | 172

♦ ♦ ♦

MEET

THE UNIFYING CONSCIOUSNESS TAROT

Welcome to *The Unifying Consciousness Tarot*. We greet you with a Salutation of Love.

This deck is a cocreation between a spiritual artist and a practical mystic. Leo Scopacasa is the founder of Orbital Arts Gallery, and I'm Lori Lytle, also known as Inner Goddess Tarot.

I discovered Orbital Arts Gallery when Tarot was my secret passion. I was living in Toronto and pursuing my second master's degree. Every day I'd savor my walk home through Kensington Market, an unpolished gem of a neighborhood, filled with galleries and graffiti, vintage clothing stores and fruit stalls, and the mouth-watering scent of street food.

One day while meandering through the market, I was stopped in my tracks by an All-Seeing Eye. It was hanging above a storefront, this large painting of an eye, floating in the cosmos over windows that were bright and alive with artwork. Everything seemed to be moving, swaying, and calling me over. This was my first connection with Orbital Arts Gallery.

Out front, I saw a small, round table for sale—it was meant for me! The top of the table was a spectacular collage of the head of Medusa, and it brought me to life. Though I was already overloaded with textbooks, I bought that table and somehow managed to lug it home. I'm so grateful that I did because more than twenty years later, I still read Tarot cards on my magickal Medusa.

While I may not remember the exact details of that day, I'll never forget the feeling, the significance and synchronicity. Leo's artwork had uplifted and so deeply resonated with my soul. In Leo, I found a kindred spirit who radiates love, compassion, and peace. He made me feel welcome and so confident that I was in the right place at the right time.

I've returned to Orbital Arts Gallery many times over the years. Leo has made some amazing pieces for me, and I keep my Tarot cards in treasure boxes that he's created. Still, our collaboration on a Tarot deck took its own mystical time to develop. More often than not, a fixed point in the future is the result of two separate paths making their ways to that precise location in their own way, and on their own schedule.

As a reader, I have always loved the traditional Waite-Smith Tarot. Magic flows through Pamela Colman Smith's artwork. That deck started my Tarot journey. It changed my life. Although I have an extensive Tarot deck collection, startlingly so, I kept returning to the Waite-Smith Tarot. It was my comfort. It was my rock. Yet, as my experience as a reader heightened, and my understanding of the energy and essence of the cards deepened, I began opening to other possibilities. It wasn't long before I began seeing Tarot's big archetypes winking at me from Leo's artwork. It was like the All-Seeing Eye again saying, *Look here, Lori Lytle*. I knew then that if we worked together, we could create a Tarot deck that would resonate on a soul level.

Eventually, the idea became too persistent to keep to myself, and I bolted to Orbital Arts to run it past Leo. I materialized on the 22nd day of the month, which just happened to be the gallery's 22nd anniversary, and pitched a 22-card Majors-only Tarot deck because I didn't want to overwhelm Leo with grand plans for a full 78-card deck—yet. And as it turned out, Leo was already working on his own project along that same wavelength, and so he was primed and ready to dive into a cocreation of a Tarot deck. Coincidence? Not a chance! I really think the universe had a hand in the divine timing of this visit.

As with any collaboration, *The Unifying Consciousness Tarot* was born from the combination of our respective arts, perspectives, philosophies, and spiritual experiences. Although our approaches were different, they blended in a kind of artistic alchemy to create our heart of gold, *The Unifying Consciousness Tarot.*

Leo is an artist. He opened Orbital Arts as his studio and gallery in 1997 with a mission to create art that helps awaken us to the understanding that we're all connected, and that universal spiritual love is our true nature. Leo says that he channels universal love through his art as a gift from his heart, and that this vibration of love is embedded in every one of his creations. He believes that everyone can access this energy simply by viewing his art. Leo refers to his work as Activation Art.

I'm a Tarot reader and a teacher. I've been carrying around a deck of cards since I was 13 years old. After many years of keeping my passion and skills to myself, I quit a joyless office job to pursue this path professionally. I'm an introvert, empath, big nerd, solitary witch, High Priestess, Gemini, overthinker, and devotee of cats and cards. My approach to the Tarot is both mystical and practical. I see the Tarot as a source of inspiration, a means of connection with the divine, as well as a tool that we can use every day to make our lives happier in the here and now.

Leo's art has the power to activate the soul of the viewer in a passive way, through achieving resonance with the inherent vibration of love. My intention was to incorporate and translate this energy into the form and structure of a Tarot deck, so that spiritual seekers can also use it actively as a tool for wisdom, empowerment, and transformation. The result is a Tarot deck that begins its healing work from the moment that it's held.

We rooted *The Unifying Consciousness Tarot* in the belief that we're all one, and we're eternal. We come from and return to the same Source energy, and that Source is LOVE. We're beings of light, but occasionally we choose to incarnate into the physical world to experience life. We come back here to learn, play, triumph, have our hearts broken, and, most of all, love. We learn how to love ourselves, and to love others, and to know that we're loved.

I believe that our experience of life is a combination of fate and free will. I personally don't believe that everything in our lives is set in stone and prearranged. What fun would that be? And yet, I also believe that we map out some aspects of our journey before we come into our physical forms, and that there are eternal parts of us that return with every incarnation. We choose some of the experiences that we want to have, and the rest unfolds as a result of how we approach our world, see ourselves and others, make decisions, and respond to whatever Fate throws our way.

Life is an epic adventure, and we exist as the mythic heroes of our own story, but when the going gets challenging in this world of form, it's easy to lose the connection with our eternal nature. We forget who we really are, and why we chose to come back in the first place.

Source does send signs and messages to help guide us, but it isn't always easy to see or hear them through the clouds and noise of our daily lives. Often, we tune out our inner whispers or second-guess our intuition, just when we need it the most. During these troubled times, we can feel small, separate, and directionless and, most distressingly, unable to connect with or rely on our own wise inner counsel. As a result, the course of our lives can become rerouted by fear and feelings of inadequacy.

The Unifying Consciousness Tarot was designed to help you access universal consciousness and that pool of infinite wisdom, compassion, and love. It will not only open your All-Seeing Eye and unlock your heart, but also your soul memory, that part of your Eternal Self that remembers everything and is capable of recognizing the way forward.

We would love for you to get to know these cards on a personal level and discover how you're meant to work with them. While they can be used like any other Tarot deck, we're confident that they'll soon reveal their unique and gentle superpowers.

◆ ◆ ◆

THE ANATOMY OF

THE UNIFYING CONSCIOUSNESS TAROT

You're about to meet a cosmic crew of otherworldly and divine beings, animals, humans, and free-form entities, all living in a universe based on the Waite-Smith Tarot structure. All the cards are fully illustrated, and the deck is suitable for Tarot beginners as well as seasoned readers. There are 79 cards in total. In addition to the traditional 56 Minor Arcana and Court Cards, the Major Arcana are featured in surprising and intriguing new forms. We can't wait for you to meet our own Arcana 22, Activation.

Can't you just feel your All-Seeing Eye beginning to open?

All the cards have sacred geometry woven through their images and backgrounds to remind us that we're all part of the same Source energy. We're woven into the divine structure and symmetry of the universe, where we play valuable and necessary roles.

The four suits of the Minor Arcana are linked with the four elements: Wands/Fire, Cups/Water, Swords/Air, and Pentacles/Earth. In addition to the sacred geometry that flows through these cards, you'll also notice that each of the Minors includes a 3-D shape floating through the card's familiar scene. You may recognize these shapes as Plato's solids, and they're thought to be the harmonious and symmetrical building blocks of our reality. Each of these shapes is a physical representation of the four elements. Wands are represented by the tetrahedron, Cups by the icosahedron, Swords by the octahedron, and Pentacles by the hexahedron or cube. The Major Arcana is linked with the most enigmatic Platonic solid, the dodecahedron. This represents the element of Aether or Spirit, the star stuff of which we're all made. This shape also appears on Arcana 22, Activation, our new trump and the card that brings our Major Arcana full circle.

As you'll see, we've also renamed the Court Cards in an effort to equalize gender and hierarchy, and to express more of the core vibration of each of these familiar roles. Pages have become Soul, Knights are Spirit, Queens are Heart, and Kings are Mind.

The Unifying Consciousness Tarot wasn't designed to be read with reversals. The cards encompass a rich and diverse range of meanings and should express the full story in their upright positions. However, if reversals resonate with you, by all means, use them. When a card is turned over, the image on the card back won't reveal the orientation of the cards waiting to be flipped.

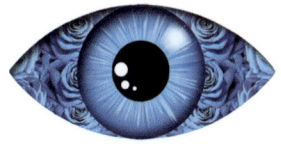

Now, dear readers, Leo and I have a special surprise for you.

Light a candle and get comfortable. It's time to acquaint yourself with the energy of our deck and introduce yourselves to one another. Leo and I invite you to look at the back of our cards. The image that you see here is a portal. It will allow you to access the deepest and highest parts of yourself.

Why a blue rose? People often say that they smell roses when they're being visited by angels or helping spirits. This is one way that Spirit or Source makes itself present to us. But the blue rose doesn't exist in nature, only in the realm of spirit and imagination. It symbolizes mystery and the attainment of the impossible. It is love, truth, and beauty beyond the physical realm. When you see the blue rose, you are on the verge of profound spiritual awakening and understanding.

The blue rose blooms eternally inside the mandorla, or vesica piscis, the sacred space and time created by two overlapping circles. It represents the interconnectedness of spirit and matter, of heaven and Earth. As human beings, we're both of these things and have access to both of these worlds. They're not separate; they weave together and they're present in everything.

The sacred geometry in the background, the Flower of Life, reminds us that everything comes from the same divine source, and that we all originate from the same blueprint. By contemplating this image, you can achieve unity within yourself and union with the loving consciousness that we all share.

Right now, or when you have a quiet moment to yourself, I invite you to try this visualization. Sink into it without expectations. Don't worry if you don't get immediate results. This is just for you, and whatever unfolds unfolds. Meditation takes practice, perseverance, and faith.

Hold the card in your hand at an easy arm's length. Perhaps support your arm on your leg or place your hand on your knee, so that it feels comfortable. Looking at the image on the back of the card, let your gaze rest softly on the blue rose.

Take a moment to relax your body. Breathe deeply and feel the earth supporting you.

In your peripheral vision, be aware of the pattern of the Flower of Life. You'll feel its vibration gently, and you may hear its chime.

Focus your gaze on that central blue rose. Imagine that you can see the petals start to move, turn, unfurl.

Let your awareness flow into the center of the rose. Imagine that you're inside that space, surrounded by blue light and cradled in the soft petals. Breathe comfortably and begin to feel what it's like to be here. Does your body feel light or grounded? Does the air feel warm or cool? Stay in this safe, inviting space for as long as you like.

Do you smell anything? The delicate fragrance of the rose? Are you aware of an increase in energy around you? Do you feel the presence of a bright, beautiful energy or consciousness around you? If so, ask a question, using your inner voice. Any question is right. Don't worry if it isn't fully formed; you'll be understood.

Answers can arrive in many ways, as an inner voice, feeling, image, or strong knowing. You'll understand that it's what you need in this moment, and that more will be revealed in time. You'll also receive a wave of all-encompassing love energy and feel it flow through you. Take a moment to resonate with it and allow your own vibration to match that vibration of love.

Welcome to *The Unifying Consciousness Tarot*. You're ready for this journey.

♦ ♦ ♦

MAJOR ARCANA

Even if you've never picked up a Tarot deck until now, you'll know many of the images in the Major Arcana. They whisper to the ancient and eternal part of you. Throughout your life, they'll appear to you in dreams and memories. You've seen glimpses of them in the faces of loved ones and rivals. They exist between the covers of fairy tales and novels, and, most of all, they stare back at you from the mirror. So, when you see them in the cards, there'll be a conscious or unconscious remembrance.

The Major Arcana are archetypes that represent the totality of human experience. The cards are distillations of those energies in a form that we can understand, interpret, and hold in our hands. They represent life lessons, initiations, challenges, triumphs, and milestone experiences that teach us who we are, and what, exactly, we came here to be and do.

We're all The Fool, the card numbered zero. As we dance through our lives, we meet and interact with each of the other Major Arcana archetypes. Sometimes we embody the energies in these cards. They might appear to us in the role of a teacher, or as a significant event in our lives. We'll welcome and love some of these cards, and we'll resist, reject, and even fear some of the others. Regardless of our initial reaction, all the Major Arcana cards have valuable and healing information to share with us. Their ultimate purpose is to guide us toward a rich and meaningful existence, and to help us reach the highest vibration of love.

Tarot cards are numbered for a reason, and their progression has meaning. The Major Arcana cards begin and end with The Fool, which is zero and carries the concept of everything and nothing, pure potential, consciousness, and Spirit. In between, we have cards numbered from 1 to 21 or, as in the case of *The Unifying Consciousness Tarot*, 22.

Unlike the cards in the Major Arcana, our lives don't always progress step by step in an orderly fashion. Sometimes we experience the archetypal energies of the Major Arcana out of sequence, and sometimes we even get to see the same ones, again and again. This is because we repeat patterns until we can master the card's lesson, pass through its initiation, or transition through an event. And then, in our own mystical time, we finally graduate to the final card. Here we experience the joy of unity, connection, and spiritual activation, and we celebrate who we've become and what we've achieved. This is the vibration of love. And then, we start all over again.

In *The Unifying Consciousness Tarot*, the Major Arcana are connected with the element of Aether, which is represented by the dodecahedron, the 12-sided Platonic solid. It's the fifth element, the quintessence, Spirit, and the shape of the universe as a whole.

The descriptions for each card in the Major Arcana will allow you to immerse yourself in the card's energy, symbolism, and story. The meanings will help you interpret the cards as they appear in a full reading or daily single-card draws. Each Major also offers a blessing that you can use for meditation, journaling, or support and inspiration: carry it in your heart.

As you work with the cards, pay attention to any Major that appears for you. Consider its meaning and energy. Ask why it's showing itself to you. Why in this particular moment? Now open up your view and discover where the card resides in the whole sequence and story of the Major Arcana. Does your card place you at the beginning of a journey, somewhere in the middle, or close to the end? What cards lie before and after your card? Looking into the past and future of this Major card helps you zoom out and see the bigger picture. Do these cards show that you're in a position of healing that has followed a challenge, or do challenges lie ahead and lead to the key to resolution? What archetypes are surrounding and influencing The Fool? How does this affect your dance? Take inventory of where you are at the present moment, and receive all that you can from the images, the activities, the symbols, and the colors.

◆ ◆ ◆

0 ✦ FOOL

Is it foolish to leave a place of spirit and light and leap into life? Or is it divine? What role does faith play now? Each time we decide to leave the heavens and the golden realm of the sun to entrust our eternal soul to a physical body, it's to play, learn, and experience all we can in this land of form. We come to remember that we're all one, a unified consciousness, and to return to love.

When you take the first step on this journey, you're the first and last archetype in the Major Arcana, The Fool.

The soul, your soul, is a red feather, light and blown easily by the winds, but also filled with unlimited life force and passion. The soul, your soul, is also the white rose, delicate but filled with pure intention and fearless innocence.

You have a companion along the road. The white dog at your side knows that you're about to fly high, fall low, climb mountains, enjoy triumphs, and face challenges of which you're still blissfully unaware. Nevertheless, she invites you to listen to your instincts and let Spirit guide you on a new adventure.

You don't know what you're heading into, because the path is still unformed, awaiting your first and subsequent steps. You have no experience to base your expectations on. Nevertheless, you're ready to take that step in perfect faith and trust.

INTERPRETATION

The time is right to start something new. Don't overthink it or make any plans, because there's no point. When The Fool springs forward, you won't know how everything will unfold, for the path is unpredictable and fraught with surprises. Trust in yourself, and the universe, and approach your situation with acceptance: it will be perfect, no matter what. Miracles will happen, and life is meant to be experienced in all of its joy and sorrow. Feel a shiver of excitement, take a deep breath, and leap forward.

A BLESSING FROM THE FOOL

May you leap into life with both feet.

I • MAGICIAN

Feel the movement and vibration that's always around you. Cosmic wheels are spinning while celestial gears find their eternal groove, ever turning, churning, and generating a force called magic. Isn't the universe a wondrous machine?

The Magician connects with this system of energy. He sees, feels, hears, and knows it well, and he has the skill, discipline, timing, and confidence to channel this Source energy into the physical world to meet his needs. He represents the power of manifestation that lies within all of us. Like The Magician, you have access to unlimited resources and possibilities. If you can imagine it, you can create it.

The four elements swirl together in this card, water flows, fire burns, wind gusts, and leaves grow. The Magician has everything he needs to achieve his goal. Air gives him clarity of mind. Fire gives him the determination to follow his passion. Water reminds him of the healing potential of his work. Earth helps him manifest tangible change.

The ouroboros, the snake devouring its own tail, appears twice on this card. It's a symbol of infinitely renewing energy. The snakes mirror each other, meaning as above, so below: what is manifest in the energetic realm is also manifested here on Earth.

INTERPRETATION

You are magical. Right now. Just as you are. Is there something that you're holding yourself back from pursuing? Why is this? Take note of what you've already gathered: your skills, talents, experience, and knowledge. Look deeper. Is there a resource that you haven't considered? The Magician understands that you already have everything you need to achieve your desires. Revel in your own power and ability. Negative thinking expends energy unwisely. You can achieve great things if you allow the potential for success to inspire rather than overwhelm you.

A BLESSING FROM THE MAGICIAN

May you dare to work your own magic.

2 • HIGH PRIESTESS

The High Priestess sees and knows all. She travels beyond the veil, moving between light and dark, and life and death; she exists beyond the limits of time and space.

She appears to you in the form that you need most, a reflection of your deepest self. She's the bright maiden of the underworld. She's the fierce mother. She's the crone who guides you through your darkest days. She embodies all the phases of the moon—waxing, full, and waning, the cycles of shining and retreating.

The High Priestess knows your story. She follows the threads of your potential from beginning to end. Rather than reveal her knowledge to you directly, she'll activate ways for you discover these mysteries on your own. She'll lead you through an initiation, remaining still in the knowledge that the secrets and revelations you seek are contained within you.

The scroll that adorns the throat of The High Priestess is unrolled for you to see, but you won't be able to read what's written—yet. In time, all will be revealed. First, you must embark on your own journey into the mysteries. She will open doors of initiation, but it's up to you to step across the threshold. There's so much more to your experience of life than what you currently perceive. Will you step through into her portal and embrace the great mystery?

INTERPRETATION

You already know the answer to your question. When The High Priestess appears, she's inviting you to believe in yourself and to trust that, ultimately, you're your own best source of wisdom. She's a sign that you're ready to explore your psychic gifts, and to embark on a spiritual path that will take you deep within yourself. You know that your intuition is strong. Now's the time to get to know it well, understand how it speaks to you, and allow it to guide you. In terms of more-mundane matters, rely on your clear perception and powers of observation to see the truth of every situation. When secrets and revelations reveal themselves to you, keep them to yourself.

A BLESSING FROM THE HIGH PRIESTESS

May you believe in yourself.

3 • EMPRESS

The Empress is the loving consciousness that flows through our physical world. She supports and sustains the growth of every living thing on Earth, offering you a world with endless opportunities for love and pleasure.

She's embedded in your earliest memories as the Great Mother who guided you into your own physical form. She's Gaia and Venus and rules over the cycles of renewal, life, death, and rebirth. We all worship her and know that she supports us through our wildness, raw beauty, appetites, and frailty.

The eyes of The Empress emerge from the vesica piscis, the womb of the universe and the channel between Spirit and matter. Her third eye is the Flower of Life, showing you that all life is connected and comes from the same pattern. Within the flower are pomegranate seeds, reminding you that life comes from death, and death comes from life.

The Empress wears a celestial crown; her dominion includes everything under heaven and Earth. She rules, but with love. She takes responsibility for every creature in her care, and she'll intervene when the balance of nature is disrupted. She asks you to see the world through the lens of love, and to be sure that your actions contribute to growth, abundance, and the elevation of all things.

INTERPRETATION

The Empress is the Mother Goddess, and like her, you take care of everyone in your world. A lot of your energy goes toward protecting your loved ones, and it brings you joy when they are happy and healthy. This is a beautiful part of who you are, but it's not all. The Empress is also the Goddess of Love, and you have that same passion and creative power within you. She invites you to connect with your divine feminine side and attract pleasure and ease into your life. Anything you focus your energy on now will flourish, so surround yourself with nature, art, music, or whatever makes life feel lush. Appreciate your strength, beauty, and resilient body. You can nurture others while also lavishing compassion and care on yourself. In fact, if you do, there's a blessing there for you: you'll have more energy to share with others.

A BLESSING FROM THE EMPRESS

May your life be abundant.

4 • EMPEROR

The Emperor rules and maintains the structure of our physical world. Drawing on Source energy, he designs rock-solid patterns that give the world order, protection, beauty, and inclusivity. We're all bound by the universal laws set out by The Emperor, and sometimes this feels as heavy as his golden crown. But once we understand how his laws work, we can create the life that we desire by working within those supportive constructs.

Firmly, but masterfully, The Emperor regulates the flow of energy of this world grid. The carnelian at the center of the grid contains his fiery ambition and courage. It's the battery that he continuously monitors and charges.

The Emperor's scepter is made of birch, a strong but flexible wood that can bend without breaking. Birch also represents new beginnings and renewal, suggesting that The Emperor isn't *always* set in his ways.

Ram's horns flank The Emperor's crown, showing his tenacious endurance and ability to push through all obstacles and opponents.

The Emperor is benevolent, but he must be obeyed. He understands that the structure of the universe must be upheld for the greater good of all. If you break his laws in the spirit of careless self-service, there will be consequences. The Emperor never relaxes his control because he's aware that the reckless actions of one can have far-reaching consequences for others.

INTERPRETATION

You're the boss. It's good to be in charge, but it also brings the weight of responsibility. You do the things that no one else wants to do. You make the difficult decisions and say *no* more often than *yes*. It's a thankless job, but there's reward enough in a job well done. Effective leadership also depends on the self-discipline of the leader who must lead by example and follow their own rules. By channeling the energy of The Emperor, you can bring order to a chaotic situation, lay the foundation for future prosperity, and mentor those who need your wisdom. If you find yourself in the role of The Emperor's subject, adhere to the rules—and learn. You can gain advantage by increasing the value of your contributions.

A BLESSING FROM THE EMPEROR

*May your actions be of benefit
to others.*

5 • HIEROPHANT

There are messages from Source all around you, and they feel electric. You can sense the compassionate eye of the universe watching over you. Sometimes, the sensory overload of the physical world makes it difficult to receive incoming signals at full capacity.

During these times, The Hierophant turns up as a wise guide who can teach you how to receive these messages. Can you put your ego aside, admit that you don't know what you don't know, and accept him as your teacher? If you do, he will open your eyes to greater realities and help you arrive at your own understanding of the cosmos and your sacred place within it.

The Hierophant appears here in the shape of our pineal gland, our Third Eye, the seat of our soul. This reminds you that you're already able to communicate with Spirit. But, if you need guidance on how to fully open those doors, he'll reveal what you need to know, and give you the keys you need.

The Sri Yantra symbolizes that the Divine is within all of us, and that the structure of the universe relies on the balance of both the masculine and feminine.

INTERPRETATION

They say when the student is ready, the teacher will appear. When The Hierophant appears, he's willing to unlock the mysteries for you, and to share his traditional and time-honored wisdom. Still, he expects that you'll also question what you learn, so that you can journey farther than his conventional boundaries. The lesson of The Hierophant is to evaluate the role that tradition and acceptable ways of thinking, behaving, or feeling play in your own life and development. Is there a limiting belief system that requires your attention? The Hierophant also steps forward when he believes that it's your turn to take on the mantle of teacher. How can you activate the evolution of others?

A BLESSING FROM THE HIEROPHANT

May you be a powerful receiver of divine messages and sacred wisdom.

6 ✦ LOVERS

The snakes whisper their truth. Their role in this sacred garden is to deliver you from evil, and to teach you to love so deeply that the universe will expand and unfurl before you. Eat their apple and also gain the knowledge of how worthy of love you are.

Love takes on an infinite number of forms. It's a force that drives, feeds, and constantly renews. Love manifests as a relationship with a partner, soulmate, or lover, a sublime connection that elevates and brings meaning to life. But the most transformational power of love doesn't come from seeking love outside yourself; it comes from finding love within.

How can you do this? Look at the harmonious pattern that is revealed in the face of the figure on The Lovers card. This symmetry permeates every being in our universe, including you. The Lovers has a simple message: you are connected with all that is, while being perfectly whole within yourself. The unifying consciousness of love flows through all of us.

INTERPRETATION

When The Lovers invite you into their sacred garden, it's time to look at the experience of love in your life. How are you giving or receiving love, within the context of either a romance, friendship, family, self, or your fellow humanity? When offered the apple, what choice are you making?

Let the universe know that you're worthy of love. Believe it, and it is so. If you're in a relationship, regardless of the current dynamic, value this union as a gift and open your eyes and heart to the inherent lessons that your soul is meant to learn from this connection. If you're seeking a loving relationship, The Lovers are here to tell you that a key and karmic partnership is forming. But above all, love yourself first and well, because your relationship with self greatly affects your powers of attraction.

The Lovers card may also herald the need to make an important decision, with a lasting outcome. Remember love heals fear. Make decisions that are in alignment with your highest vibration.

A BLESSING FROM THE LOVERS

*May love be the guiding force
of your life.*

7 • CHARIOT

The Chariot is the call of the open road, the lure of new discoveries, and longing for unfamiliar sights. It arrives when you know in your bones that there's somewhere else you need to be, and there's more to gain if you just go after it. The cosmos is inviting you to awaken, enliven, and take your place in the spiral dance.

The path into the vortex of movement and momentum is flanked by sphinxes, magical and wise creatures. They're waiting for you to answer this one question: "Where are you going?" If you can't articulate or visualize this clearly, they won't let you pass. How can you reach your destination if you don't really know where that is? If you're being spun in different directions, you'll need to resolve that conflict in either your mind or heart. Once you can get clear on your destination and lock in a target, they'll gladly give you the signal to GO.

INTERPRETATION

Have confidence in your capabilities. When The Chariot has arrived, there's no place for self-doubt or complacency. It signals that you're up for a challenge, and ready to go farther than you'd imagined. Chances are, you're already experiencing a restlessness that's conveying a message to get going. If you focus on what you want, and where you want to be, you'll get there. Trust in your ability to navigate any detours or unexpected forks in the road along the way.

A BLESSING FROM THE CHARIOT

*May you be the driving force
of your own life.*

8 • STRENGTH

It takes Strength and courage to live in this world. Sometimes you must be as sweet as a rose, or as fierce as a lion, depending on the challenge that you're currently facing. Situations will test your patience, fear will cause you to lash out and roar, and ultimately there will be opportunities to emerge transformed like a butterfly. Being human requires that you trust that your Strength will never run out, because it will always renew itself through your connection to divine source. Otherwise, what's the alternative?

When life sends you formidable challenges, having the presence of mind to hold your ground and show love in the face of aggression is greater than victory won through force. When you learn to access your heart's resilience, grace, and Strength, your baser instincts can be tamed. Activate a divine perspective, and you'll have the power to transform any situation from conflict to harmony.

INTERPRETATION

You're strong. You have to be. You're dealing with challenges that test your patience, perseverance, and compassion, but now's not the time to give up. Strength wants you to know that you have deeper resources within yourself and they're ready to support you—if you can find it in your heart to support them. When facing an external challenge, shine an extra-bright light within to ensure that you've resolved any internal conflict. Tame and heal your own inner beasts so that you can control the situation instead of letting it control you. You're capable of getting things to where you need them to be, in the kindest, most diplomatic way. This is the divine path of Strength.

A BLESSING FROM STRENGTH

*May your compassion inform
your strength.*

9 • HERMIT

The Hermit is at home in lonely places. His purpose in life is the pursuit of the wisdom that comes from deep introspection, and he needs solitude and seclusion. It takes strength and bravery for The Hermit to venture into the cosmos of the soul. He may get lost there, or be tempted to stay in this dark, liminal place of endless discovery. He knows that his wisdom can't benefit others if he doesn't resurface to share it, so he always leaves a light on to guide him back home.

The Hermit holds a lantern high above the mountains. He's the lighthouse that guides you through perils encountered along your own spiritual journey as a seeker of wisdom. His flame is balanced on the point of a smoky quartz tower to keep you practical and grounded. The information that you gain during this time will be used as a catalyst for future growth.

INTERPRETATION

The one person that you can't escape is yourself, so it's important to enjoy your own company. Appreciate your alone time. Make it sacred. Use this time to get to know who you are, what you care about, and what you really think. Explore your rich inner world: read, write, and go to those quiet, peaceful places that make you happy.

If you're feeling the need to take a break from accommodating others, do so without apology. You'll discover more valuable and healing insight within you at this time.

A BLESSING FROM THE HERMIT

May you grow wise in your own company.

10 • WHEEL OF FORTUNE

Just when you think you're in control, fate has a way of turning everything upside down. Life is a spinning wheel; it is magnificent and mystifying, a game that will send you in constant pursuit of answers and meaning. The trick is to enjoy the mysteries and surprises that fate sends you, without feeling the need to explain them all away. What fun would it be if you already had everything figured out?

When The Wheel of Fortune appears in your cards, luck is on your side. It gives you a glimpse into the bigger pattern and cycles that underlie your daily life. If you look closely, it will reveal how past actions are now affecting the present, and reminds you how quickly fortunes can change.

Do you remember the Sphinx that appeared on The Chariot card? Here she is again, asking you a question: In this moment, are you subject to fate or do you have free will? The answer lies somewhere in between. You're part of a divine structure, represented by the elemental shapes, the Platonic solids, that the Sphinx shows you. But, within that structure you have the freedom to choose, create, and change, just as the wheel above her spins.

INTERPRETATION

Life is change. You're up, then down, then back up again. Just as you find your center, you get thrown for a loop. All you can do while fate spins the wheel is to roll with it and enjoy the ride. Hang on too tightly and you'll get thrown. And even when events feel random and out of your direct control, trust that there is a deeper meaning. You might not see the bigger picture at the moment, but The Wheel of Fortune confirms that there's divine providence at play. Make the most of the serendipitous opportunities that cross your path.

A BLESSING FROM THE WHEEL OF FORTUNE

May you befriend Fate's spinning wheel.

II • JUSTICE

Justice presides over the cosmos with her third eye wide open. She's asking you to look at yourself with an All-Seeing Eye. In order to gain clarity on a current situation, you'll need to weigh your beliefs and past experiences and stand accountable for your wise or foolish actions. Have you been acting in alignment with your truth? Are the karmic scales of Justice seesawing from right to left or are they perfectly balanced?

Before Justice reaches a verdict, she makes sure that she's contemplated all the evidence and circumstances truthfully. True Justice derives from universal law, tenets that are older and deeper than those created by humankind. Knowing the interconnectedness of all things, Justice requires all of us to take responsibility for our actions. She is the keeper of cause and effect and monitors how your choices add or take away from the greater good and balance.

Justice brandishes the unwavering sword of truth, bound by her conviction to uphold the universal laws. The tip of the sword hits the bull's eye, because Justice is unerring and always gets to the heart of the matter. The hilt rests on petrified wood, a substance that records our stories and histories throughout the ages so that nothing is forgotten.

INTERPRETATION

You have significant decisions to make that will require a rational rather than an emotional approach. Before you commit to a course of action, Justice asks that you take time out to analyze what's important to you, and why. Why do you feel, act, or think the way you do? What's motivating your actions or reactions? Gaining an honest knowledge of self will help you make decisions that are more aligned with your path. Choosing an inauthentic way forward might feel right in the moment but will invariably tip Justice's scales the wrong way in time.

A BLESSING FROM JUSTICE

May your scales balance.

12 • HANGING ONE

The Hanging One arrives to give us a new perspective. He knows that the physical world is beautiful and his physical form is precious, and that both provide many opportunities for pleasure and pain. But he never forgets that he is made of stars and things eternal. A whole universe exists within him.

When things turn out to be different than they appear, and the world turns topsy-turvy, The Hanging One smiles, relaxes into it, and embraces the new view. Reality is subjective, after all, and he can see his world from any angle he chooses.

Reversal and resistance are sometimes signs that you need to stop and wait. The Hanging One knows when to hang back, so that he can become a conduit for information that needs a safe place to land. He keeps his eyes and mind open and remembers that he alone has the ability to make his life a prison or a paradise. He's on a path toward a deeper understanding of the universe, so he shifts his perspective and yields to this new experience.

INTERPRETATION

There's nothing to do in this moment but surrender control and let things unfold. Don't waste energy trying to push a situation ahead; the timing isn't right. If things aren't quite coming together as expected, there's a good reason, the details of which are more likely to arrive once you're able to turn a situation on its head.

In the meantime, challenge yourself to see beyond established patterns of thinking and old stories. This period of reflection will bring illumination and the potential of a key breakthrough. Releasing control may feel like you're having to make a sacrifice, but that's the point when The Hanging One has activated this time of suspension. What are you being asked to release?

A BLESSING FROM THE HANGING ONE

May you surrender to epiphany.

13 ♦ DEATH

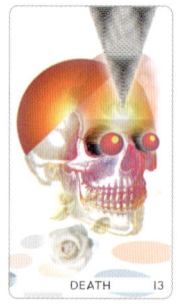

Death is a quiet companion throughout your life, reminding you that while energy is eternal, you have only a finite amount of time in this human form. With Death looming on the physical horizon, life is as ephemeral as a rose. Sweeter, more precious and sacred. Death asks you how you are using your time here. Are you aware of your surroundings? Are your senses alive with color, scent, sound, and texture? What do you love? How deeply do you love?

The goal of existence is transformation, and although it doesn't always feel like this, it's also the reward. When you meet Death in the cards, he will take you down to your bare bones before he raises and builds you up into a stronger, more eternal version of yourself. Death brings necessary endings as well as new beginnings.

Death sees the world beyond the illusion of the physical with his all-seeing third eye. He appreciates the sunrise and the sunset and asks that you take the time to stop and smell the white rose.

INTERPRETATION

Death brings transformation, a cessation of what *was*, with no turning back. He brings solutions, resolutions, heartache, relief, and unexpected, secretly desired and necessary endings. He also brings the promise of bright, new beginnings. With this card, you can expect a significant change in your life. If you fight or try to hold on to the past, the transition will be more difficult than it needs to be.

This card can seem formidable when it shows up with its heavy message of metaphorical death. Change or anything that presents as an initiation can be scary, especially when it wasn't your first choice. Death is Spirit sending you an opportunity to grow, and once you've passed through this transition or transformation and let go of the old, tired, or toxic, you'll be ready to start an exciting new phase of existence.

A BLESSING FROM DEATH

May letting go bring transformation.

14 • TEMPERANCE

Having made your way successfully through the valley of the shadow of Death in the previous card (13), you've arrived at a peaceful refuge in Temperance, and you're greeted by twin angels. You know your ultimate goal lies farther down the road, but you can rest here for a while, to rebalance and heal and to get ready for further challenges ahead.

The massive wings and glowing aura of the angels remind you that you're in the presence of celestial beings, but their nakedness is reassuring because it gives them a human physicality. They focus their attention on two golden cups and regulate the flow of water between them. That water flows in a way that shouldn't be possible according to the scientific laws of our universe, and yet angels do the impossible with serenity. Not a drop is lost or cast off. The water just flows.

Contrast exists in balance and blends together in the world of Temperance. Nothing is jarring here; nothing takes precedence over anything else. The angels represent the two contrasting sides of one being, flowing and existing in harmony. The rainbow holds the watery infinity loop in place and becomes the bridge that connects you to source energy.

INTERPRETATION

Temperance is about balance and moderation in all things. No extremes. No drama. While the Death card asks you to let go of or end something in your life, Temperance doesn't make these demands.

Temperance invites you to create the outcome that you desire by recombining all the resources that you have at your disposal. Recognize where things may be stressed or amplified or neglected, and shift them around so that they flow with greater ease. Your new, natural rhythm will be achieved through a process of trial and error. Give yourself the time to find the solutions that work best.

A BLESSING FROM TEMPERANCE

May you find flow.

15 ♦ DEVIL

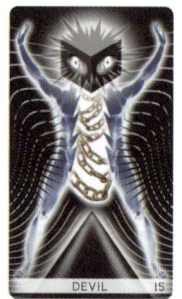

Whenever it's a struggle to connect with Source, it manifests as a feeling or an experience of isolation and separation. This is the energy and the lesson of The Devil. He'll convince you that you're helpless, trapped, and worthless. You can see what's going on, but still you think there's no way out. You want to look and walk away, but he keeps your focus on him because he's very attractive. The Devil binds you with chords of fright, limitation, illusion, and confusion. You can't think straight, and you forget who you really are.

Once you realize that you're your own Devil, the designer of your own traps and prisons, you have the ability to set yourself free and become whole again. No one else can do that for you. When you can remember that you're worthy and have a role to play in the grand scheme of things, your soul will welcome you home.

INTERPRETATION

You aren't as trapped or powerless as you think. The Devil arrives whenever you're in the grip of an unhappy or unhealthful situation, person, or state of being. Now is the time to start cutting his chains. It's tempting to stay where you are, certainly easier and more comfortable or familiar, but it's draining your vitality and joy. Summon the courage to look your demon in the eyes. Don't listen to that voice that tells you can't, whether it's your own fear or the voice of someone in your life. Choose to set yourself free.

A BLESSING FROM THE DEVIL

May you free yourself from that which binds.

16 • TOWER

You maneuver around your own life's chessboard, certain that you understand your role and the rules of play. When The Tower appears, the game changes, suddenly and unpredictably. Just when you're feeling secure, another piece attacks, or fate knocks you off the board and you find yourself in free fall.

When your strategy and security blow up, how will you respond? Will you hit the ground running? Or will you concede—game over?

The Tower looks imposing and solid on the outside, but it's crumbling from within. It has to come down, but you don't have to be trapped inside and crushed when it does. This chaotic and potentially apocalyptic archetype will put you into a free fall. Your ego, comfort, and control will feel shattered by this bolt from the blue. The Tower brings an experience of total freedom and release from who you think you are, and from whatever is holding you back from living your soul's truth. Once the dust settles, you'll need both feet planted firmly on the ground so that you can start rebuilding. Stronger this time. More eternal.

INTERPRETATION

Pressure is building in some area of your life, and a situation is unstable. Sudden change is disruptive and shocking, but something has to give. If your Tower has already crumbled, and you've been in free fall for a while, allow yourself to hit the ground running. Any attempt to avoid the reality of an undesirable situation only prolongs pain and growth. Your power in these situations lies in being able to adapt and adjust, knowing that you'll be able to rebuild in a way that suits you much better. It may take some time, but you'll understand.

A BLESSING FROM THE TOWER

May you trust in your power to bounce back.

17 • STAR

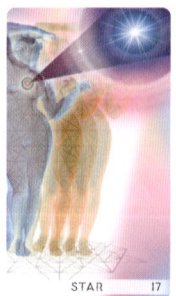

You've been holding your breath, tense for some time. The Star arrives like an exhale, a release, relaxation. In the sequence of the Major Arcana, The Star appears after extremely challenging cards. It follows the rollercoaster of Death to Temperance, and The Devil to The Tower. This is the calm after a storm, and healing after events that shook your faith in yourself and the world. The Star is the embodiment of peace and grace.

When life is at its darkest, The Star reminds you that you're luminous. And as such, you'll always have a way back to the light. Dare to hope. Make a wish. Whisper a prayer. The Star shines her light into the night to guide anyone who has lost their way.

INTERPRETATION

You've been through difficult times, and it may feel like you've lost track of who you are at your core. The Star is a homecoming. You've returned to yourself. Be gentle with yourself. Take time to heal and replenish and know that nothing needs your attention as much as this. When you're ready, you can take your place as the star of your own life, on your own terms.

When The Star appears, divine guidance is available to you. Ask for it and watch for signs and synchronicities. There's hope in the situation around you right now. Have faith that things will work out as they should.

A BLESSING FROM THE STAR

May you return to Self and shine like the star you are.

18 • MOON

When The Moon rises, so do emotions. The Moon activates something ancient and primal within you, and it can be unsettling to realize that there's much more to life than what you experience during the light of day.

The Moon stirs things up. She draws up and out what you prefer to keep down and in. She can provoke fear and temporary wildness and madness when she's in her full power. And yet, you must love and welcome her because you are her.

The Moon revolves through cycles and phases. She knows that nothing is permanent, and that life is a constant state of flux, waxing and waning. There is much to be learned from honoring the cycles of nature and recognizing them in yourself, rather than trying to bend divine timing to your will. The Moon reveals her wisdom only when, like her, you're in the right phase.

The wolf is the primal force and instinctual knowing that lies within you. It's curled up, waiting to emerge when its dark and quiet. It wants to howl.

INTERPRETATION

You're not tame. You're ancient and eternal. You've been through every archetypal experience and through every incarnation, and those memories are stored deep within you. Reach out to your ancestral knowing and let your intuition guide you. This wisdom doesn't always find expression in words; it often appears in visions, dreams, and meditation, so look for it in these forms.

The Moon invites you to journey into your own shadow. Her path isn't for the faint of heart, but the healing and growth that you seek will come from shining a light on your fears and embracing your darkness.

A BLESSING FROM THE MOON

May The Moon light your way through the shadow.

19 • SUN

The Sun is pure joy. It feels like a flower unfurling and blossoming after the winter. It's you awakening to the full glory of who you really are. After your journey through challenges and shadowy places, you can turn your face up to the bright, shining sun and know the bliss of simply being alive.

The white-hot light at the center of The Sun pulls you into pure Source energy. Immerse yourself in its radiance, and you'll experience the ecstasy of eternity and infinite expansion.

The light and warmth of The Sun sustains all life on Earth. The Sun hides nothing. It holds nothing back. It pulses with all of its power. It is a source of joy that everyone can access simply by looking up.

INTERPRETATION

The Sun brings a simple message: Be happy. Life is good. You've done a lot of soul searching, but now you can leave the shadows behind and anticipate bright times ahead. Receive all the blessings that the world has to offer you with gratitude and trust in your deservedness. It's time to have some fun. Go ahead and do what lights you up and makes you feel like a kid again.

When The Sun shines in your cards, you're heading into a time of success, recognition, and appreciation for who you are, and all that you do. Let yourself be seen, show your talents, and be the brightest light in the room. Activate your solar energy. When you radiate positivity and joy into the world, you'll also draw it back to you.

A BLESSING FROM THE SUN

*May you joyfully receive
all blessings.*

20 • JUDGEMENT

JUDGEMENT 20

Judgement brings a message. Your life has become too small for you. You needed time in your shell to learn and develop, and now it's time to crack it wide open and grow. You're ready to emerge.

In your life, you'll be it all: success and failure, kindness and cruelty, folly and wisdom. You've erred, and you've made mistakes, for that's what it is to be human. Judgement arrives with the offer of a second chance. All she asks is that you forgive yourself—and move on. Crack through the confinement of personal judgment. It's time to make peace with all that was, and in doing so, step back into alignment with your calling, and all that may be.

The angel is symbolic of our eternal form. It has blue morpho butterfly wings, representing transformation, and the presence of the guiding Divine. The egg is the reality that we create for ourselves. It's the place where we can feel safe as we prepare to grow and ascend. The eye is our spiritual awareness that allows us to see our infinite potential. The Merkabah that hovers above the angel is the vehicle that will transport our consciousness to higher realms.

INTERPRETATION

What's your calling? Are you living it? If not, why not? This is your cosmic wake-up call to rise, expand, and align with your purpose. Judgement asks you to reflect on the past, what you wish you did and didn't do, and then let them go. It's time to leave those formative experiences behind and move forward with trust in the evolution of a higher judgment.

A BLESSING FROM JUDGEMENT

*May you answer the call
of your soul.*

21 ♦ WORLD

What a journey it's been. You started with an inexperienced and foolish heart, and now everything has come to a perfect state of completion. You've found your place in The World. You've achieved what you set out to do. Take this moment to celebrate all that you've accomplished and have become. The World arrives to say congratulations: you've learned how to use your time on Earth well.

From this vantage point, you can see the truth of existence, that it's an upward spiral. The wreath around the world shows your earthly success. The minute one journey is completed, the next adventure begins, and, once again, you become The Fool. The infinity symbol reminds you that there's no end, and the cycle of life, death, and rebirth is eternal. The wings carry you to the next level of experience because the ultimate goal is the flight, the journey. The World wants you to understand that you create our own world, and your experience of it.

INTERPRETATION

Take a moment to pat yourself on the back for a job well done. Then get ready to move on. As this cycle of your life or a situation reaches success and completion, another is getting ready to begin. Focus on the details that allow this to end seamlessly, so that you can move on to your next chapter unencumbered by loose threads. Contemplate your next journey with the openness of The Fool, yet applying the master strokes honed by The World.

A BLESSING FROM THE WORLD

May you create the world your heart and soul desire.

22 • ACTIVATION

The Blue Rose appears when you've gone beyond the known world. This blossom doesn't exist in nature, only in the realm of spirit and imagination. It symbolizes the attainment of the impossible, the existence of the improbable, and lets you know that anything that you can envision is now possible for you.

The All-Seeing Eye floats in the pool of infinite wisdom, compassion, and love that we all come from and return to. It remembers everything, activates your soul memory, and shows you the way forward. The Unifying Consciousness of Love sees you, and Source welcomes you back home.

The Blue Rose is held by the dodecahedron, the shape of the universe, the element of Aether or Spirit, confirming that harmony underlies all things. It's a state to which we can all aspire and achieve.

INTERPRETATION

With all that you've dreamed, felt, and experienced during your journey through life, and through the Major Arcana, things are different. Now, it's crystal clear that everything comes back to love. Love is the force that unifies us; it's the Unifying Consciousness that we all share.

The Blue Rose appears with a message from Spirit. You're on the verge of profound spiritual awakening and understanding. You've attained a deep knowing that we're all connected, that we all come from and return to the same divine Source. Now it's time to activate that wisdom and let it be the force that informs your experiences going forward.

What does it mean to be guided by love? If you operate under the assumption that we're all connected and worthy of love and blessings, does your world shift for you? Are you ready to become The Fool again, this time with wisdom and memory, and start out on your journey with compassion and trust?

A BLESSING FROM ACTIVATION

May you be guided by the Unifying Consciousness of Love.

MINOR ARCANA

The Minor Arcana have a different kind of power than the Majors. The Minors are stepping-stones between the universal forces and revelations of the Majors. They represent the beauty and challenges of daily life, and the small joys that make every day worth living. You have more control over the situations that you encounter in the Minor Arcana, and these cards are there to help you with your Major Arcana experiences.

The Minor Arcana cards are numbered from Ace to Ten and have four Court Cards. They are divided into four suits: Wands, Cups, Swords, and Pentacles. Each of these suits represents an aspect of the human experience, and they have their own personality and characteristics. To help you relate to and understand these suits, they're linked to one of the four basic elements: fire, water, air, and earth.

You'll notice that each suit of *The Unifying Consciousness Tarot's* Minors also includes a 3-D shape that's floating somewhere in the card's scene. These shapes are Plato's solids. Each solid relates to one of the four elements, and they're thought to be the harmonious and symmetrical building blocks of our reality. Their presence lets you know that there's always potential to guide a situation to an outcome that allows for positive transformation for you or the person you're reading for.

To get to know the Minor Arcana, first get familiar with the suits and elements. What do they signify for you? What do they evoke? Pay attention to the suits that resonate and that make you feel at home and powerful. Notice when a suit challenges or sparks resistance. Now, immerse yourself in the images. Let the symbols, colors, and pictures speak to you. The scenes in each Minor Arcana card give you a glimpse into the bigger story, so let your intuition play. Imagine that you're in that scene or are watching it unfold before you.

❖ ❖ ❖

THE SUITS AND THEIR ELEMENTS

WANDS–FIRE–TETRAHEDRON

Wands are connected to the element of fire. This is the realm of Spirit, creativity, and things that want to grow and expand. It's the fire in your belly, and the spark of the Divine within you. Wands feed your passion and ambition, give you confidence and determination, and remind you what it is to be alive. Fire is flexible and adaptable. It brings light, warmth, and inspiration, but it's also unpredictable and dangerous when it runs wild.

A wand isn't a dead stick; it's a magic wand. It's so full of life force that green leaves are bursting from its branches. The suit of Wands in *The Unifying Consciousness Tarot* is infused with the transformational power of the Violet Flame, a high-frequency violet light. Meditating on the Violet Flame raises your vibration, clears out negativity, and facilitates spiritual healing.

The tetrahedron is a four-sided pyramid that's also connected with the element of fire. This form has a flat base to support it, and its sides join and rise to a shared point that focuses energy and directs it to the heavens. Meditating on this shape encourages you to act toward your ambitions and pursue your passions.

CUPS–WATER–ICOSAHEDRON

Cups are connected to the element of water. This is the realm of emotion, intuition, and the heart. Cups represent love, relationships, and things that make you cry tears of sadness and joy. You're composed of water. You need it to live. It nurtures and cleanses you, but just as emotions can be overwhelming, water can also drown or sweep you away.

Water always finds a way to get to where it needs to be, and it's willing to take its time to loosen blockages and erode rock. Like water, love is also a human necessity. It fills your cup but can also break and harden your heart. It inspires a depth of feeling and emotions, all of which appear in the suit of Cups.

A cup is a vessel that holds space and receives. It encourages you to drink deeply and gaze within. You can transform your consciousness the same way that water will take on the shape of its vessel. *The Unifying Consciousness Tarot's* Cups are made of solid gold because it is a precious metal, and a symbol of spiritual perfection.

The icosahedron is also connected to the element of water. The faces of the icosahedron are made up of 20 equilateral triangles. This shape holds energy, rather than directing it. Meditating on this form encourages you to understand and flow with your emotions, and to make your heart your sacred sanctuary.

SWORDS–AIR–OCTAHEDRON

Swords are connected to the element of air. This is the realm of the mind, how you think, speak, and determine what you believe to be right and true. Swords represent clear thoughts, logical reasoning, articulate speech, and honesty. The element of air is seemingly intangible, but it can be experienced as either a gentle breeze or a tornado. Just like your thoughts.

Swords are powerful tools. They can be used for good or for ill, just as your mind can be your best friend or your worst enemy. Your thoughts create your world, and if you keep your thoughts in balance, a harmonious resolution to inner and outer conflict will always present itself. The cross guard on the hilt of *The Unifying Consciousness Tarot's* swords is an All-Seeing Eye that cultivates clarity of mind.

The octahedron is also connected to the element of air. Two pyramids join on a flat base, and it has eight triangular faces. The pyramids mirror each other, and energy circulates with ease between the two points. Meditating on this form helps you to see all sides of yourself with clarity, and to reflect upon and express your truth.

PENTACLES–EARTH–CUBE/HEXAHEDRON

Pentacles are connected to the element of earth. This is the realm of the body, the natural world, things that you can touch and hold and that bring you comfort and pleasure. Pentacles are practical resources, and the rewards that manifest from hard work and consistent effort. This could be a cozy place to live, a lush garden, a strong body, a good job, money in the bank, or simply the confidence in your ability to shape your physical reality into what you desire. Earth is the solid ground beneath your feet; it's slow growth and an understanding of the cycles of life and death, and the consequence of time.

A Pentacle is often represented as a shiny, gold coin. In *The Unifying Consciousness Tarot* that coin is inscribed with the Flower of Life, a design that reminds you of the interconnectedness of all that lives and grows, and of the sacred pattern to which we all belong.

The hexahedron or cube is also connected to the element of earth. It has six square faces, equal in size. It has the greatest stability of all the Platonic solids. It sits, flat on the ground, and isn't going to move or roll away without manipulation. Meditating on this form brings grounding, practical wisdom, and a connection with the supportive energy of nature.

❖ ❖ ❖

THE NUMBERS

The Minor Arcana are numbered from Ace to Ten. There are two ways to understand and work with the numbers when reading the cards, and both approaches can be used simultaneously. The first is the sequence of the numbers; the second is the inherent meaning of the number itself.

The progression of the numbers is a story. The numbers that come up in a reading let you know if you're at the beginning of something in your life, in the middle, or reaching the end. Think of the feelings you associate with beginnings, middles, and endings.

At the beginning of a relationship, a project, or a phase of life, you're excited about all the potential and possibilities. You don't know what lies ahead, but you're ready to get going. You have energy that hasn't, as of yet, been compromised by challenges. You will feel this energy in the Aces and Twos of the Minor Arcana.

When you move into the Threes and Fours, things start to come together. You've taken the potential of the Ace and manifested it into something solid and real. You've laid the foundation for future growth and feel comfortable where you are.

You face your first significant challenge in the Fives. This is the hump, the setback to navigate, the test of your resolve. If you refuse to face the Fives or can't make your peace with the situation, you won't be able to progress.

After the difficulties of the Fives, the Sixes bring a return to harmony and balance. You're wiser, and you know your capabilities. You celebrate victory.

In the Sevens and Eights, you move forward. You get better at what you're doing, and know that you're in the home stretch. Here you may pause to assess and adjust your course as necessary.

Finally, when you arrive at the Nines, you achieve a goal or reach an outcome, and you experience the intense power of the element/suit. You reach completion in the Tens, and you're already starting to move toward your next story. Feel that arc, how the energy rises from the beginning, plateaus at the middle, and then rolls with greater ease and momentum toward the ending.

Here are some key numerological concepts to start with before adding your own personal associations as you work with the cards. Make note of the appearance of numbers that you consider lucky, challenging, or personally significant, especially if they repeat throughout the reading.

ACE	✦	beginnings, potential, a gift
TWO	✦	choice, balance, partnership
THREE	✦	creation, integration, perspective
FOUR	✦	structure, stability, foundation
FIVE	✦	challenge, conflict, difficulty
SIX	✦	harmony, beauty, generosity
SEVEN	✦	adjustment, contemplation, resourcefulness
EIGHT	✦	movement, mastery, commitment
NINE	✦	culmination, intensity, integration
TEN	✦	completion, understanding, transition

✦ ✦ ✦

COURT CARDS

Over time, you'll get to know your Court Cards as friends, nemeses, and your teachers. Start with this simple premise: the Court Cards are people. And every Court Card has a unique personality and plays a role in your reading.

The traditional Court Cards aren't numbered and instead carry the ranks of Page, Knight, Queen, and King. They're usually depicted as a solitary person holding the symbol of their suit. Their age and gender are clear in older Tarot decks, and their rank places them firmly within a hierarchy. In *The Unifying Consciousness Tarot,* we've changed the names of the Court Cards. Our intention is to express the card's meaning and essence without that layer of gender or hierarchy. Each character in the Court Cards has its unique, necessary, and beautiful function. To get to know them, consider the characteristics of their suit/element, as well as their role.

❖ ❖ ❖

THE UNIFYING CONSCIOUSNESS TAROT COURT CARDS:

Pages are SOUL, the pure essence of the suit/element without experience or ego.

Knights are SPIRIT, that which drives us to action.

Queens are HEART, the source that nurtures and creates.

Kings are MIND, the thinkers, planners, and those who remember.

In most cases, the Court Cards are YOU. They reveal your role, how you're behaving in a situation, and, depending on the position in the reading, they may represent your best attitude or approach. The Court Cards are powerful for this reason, because they're showing you YOURSELF. They're giving you an outside perspective on YOU, the person you should know best but may not be seeing clearly.

The Court Cards present your strengths, talents, and capabilities. They spark memories and unravel histories and mysteries. They reveal patterns of behavior and thought that are either serving you well or may need to be shifted. And if you find that a Court Card clearly isn't representing you, it could be that someone else is showing up in the reading. This is natural if you are asking about a relationship, or family or group dynamics.

♦ ♦ ♦

HOW TO USE THE ACTIVATION

In addition to the card meanings, each Minor Arcana card offers an Activation. This is an invitation to connect with the card's unique energy, and to act on the information and inspiration that it offers you. You can use that phrase as a mantra or affirmation throughout your day, in your meditation practice, or as a prompt for journaling.

♦ ♦ ♦

WANDS

ACE OF WANDS

Divine inspiration strikes. If you've been waiting for a sign, this is it. The idea you have, the one that seems too big and glorious, if you grab on to it and run with it—it'll work. There's a new spark in your soul. Fan that flame with your passion, ambition, and creativity and it will go wild. Second-guessing yourself will smother the potential, and doubt will dampen it, so be daring instead and get excited about everything that you're about to do. The intensity of your desire may scare you, but take that first, decisive step toward your vision and you'll create the momentum you need to make things happen. You have a magic wand in your hand—go on and use it.

ACTIVATION

I'm ready to burn brightly.

TWO OF WANDS

You have the wider world in your sights. You've already created a good life for yourself, and you've accomplished a lot, but the fire in your belly is telling you that there's more out there waiting for you. There's more to discover, experience, and achieve. And that's thrilling. Are you ready to step through the portal, to leave the security of your known world and expand your horizons? Before you do, pause and clearly visualize what you want to pursue. And then, dream bigger. Widen your scope of your belief in your capabilities. Once you've become excited about your possibilities, start formulating a plan and prepare to take action.

ACTIVATION

I can create the world I desire.

THREE OF WANDS

The world is at your feet, and the universe is at your fingertips. Your plan is coming together, rooted and growing, taking on a life of its own, expanding and revealing even greater possibilities. From this high perspective you have a clear view of what life has to offer you, and now you can reach further than you initially imagined. Success lies ahead if you continue to follow your vision with both passion and strategy. You'll require patience and trust as well. Once you've set your intention in motion, keep your focus on the bigger picture and avoid the urge to micromanage its manifestation.

ACTIVATION

I'm capable of infinite expansion.

FOUR OF WANDS

Community and the company of kindred spirits are your lifeblood. You know that success is sweeter when you share it with others, and milestones and special occasions take on greater meaning when you celebrate them with people you care about. Rejoicing at the triumphs of others as if they were your own raises your vibration and feeds your own fire too. So, take advantage of reasons to celebrate and create them if necessary. Spend time with people who light you up. You're not alone. Your life intertwines with those you love like an intricate dance. You support each other, at times taking the lead, at times stepping back. By allowing yourself and the people in your life to dance in their own way, the harmony of the whole choreography is enhanced.

ACTIVATION

I'm supported by a loving community.

FIVE OF WANDS

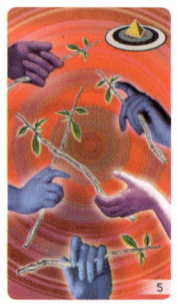

Do you feel the buzz of energy all around you? There's an urgency to get moving and working. You're geared up and ready to go, but things just aren't coming together. Until this tension is resolved, expect frustration, delays, and irritating blockages. The push and pull may be conflicting desires within yourself, or it may be coming from others in your private or professional life. The Five of Wands exposes a dynamic of competition and a struggle between different agendas fighting for dominance. In any case, don't get pulled into conflict with others or let yourself be pulled apart. Try to find some unity within yourself and common ground with others; you'll achieve more in this way. You're on the verge of creating something wonderful; let this static electricity inspire rather than frustrate you.

ACTIVATION

I turn chaos into creativity.

SIX OF WANDS

You're on course to achieve a personal victory. Feel that euphoria now, the bliss of reaching a goal, surpassing your expectations, and flying higher than you thought you could. When that success manifests, raise your arms victoriously and feel the joy of what you've accomplished. With success comes a call to leadership. Your direction is needed and will be appreciated, but it takes courage to step out of the crowd. Have confidence in your abilities and rise to the occasion. Inspire others with your optimism. If you take the lead, people will happily follow you and cheer you on while they do it.

ACTIVATION

I'm a leader.

SEVEN OF WANDS

Before you let someone into your world, take a good look at them. Will they add to your serenity or cause you stress? Are they demanding something that you don't want to give? Your time, mind, and heart are sacred. If someone is demanding access to a part of you that you don't want to share, or if they're trying to take something from you that you've worked hard to create, stop them in their tracks. Stand up for your beliefs. Stand up for yourself. The person you are and the life you have created are precious. Protect your domain and let the universe know what you're unwilling to tolerate.

ACTIVATION

*I decide who and what's allowed into
my heart, mind, and soul.*

EIGHT OF WANDS

Momentum is building, and you're on a white-knuckled, exhilarating ride that's heading toward your goal. Surrender to the speed. Urge it to go faster. At this crucial time, don't try to slow things down or throw up a wall of resistance because you don't feel ready for success and all it will bring. Remember that you set things in motion with your desires and your actions. You set the course with an inner compass that always keeps you on track. Previous challenges weren't able to defeat you, and now potentials and possibilities are coming into alignment with reality, so get out of your own way and fly toward your target at light speed. Everything you've longed and worked for lies before you; focus on that with all you have.

ACTIVATION

I release resistance and achieve my goals.

NINE OF WANDS

You've had to be strong for so long that it feels like you've turned to stone. You can't imagine what it would be like to relax your guard, and you shudder to think what would happen if you did. The losses that you've suffered in the past have caused you to harden your heart and stoically protect what remains. Right now, it will serve you to remain vigilant, but know that a time of safety will finally arrive, and you'll be able to lay down your arms and rest. You have strength left in you, and you have guardians who have your back. Your courage and perseverance will pay off.

ACTIVATION

I have come so far. I will not be defeated.

TEN OF WANDS

You're carrying too much. You have your own responsibilities, and you often take on everyone else's as well. Because you're trying so hard not to let anything slip from your grasp, you've lost sight of your ultimate goal. Can you delegate or drop some of those tasks so that you can focus on what's really important? If not, your only option is to push through to the end.

You're actually close to reaching your goal, even though you can't see it, and in truth you'll gain satisfaction from bringing everything to a tidy closure even if it tests the limits of your stamina. When you achieve what you set out to do, drop those burdens. They may be familiar companions at this point, but don't continue to carry them with you out of habit. And next time, be mindful of what you commit to, and if it's the best use of your time and energy.

ACTIVATION

I don't take on more than I can handle.

SOUL OF WANDS

You're fast, sleek, and hard to catch. You're a flitting light, a glimpse of foxfire, then on to your next adventure. Enjoy your cleverness and confidence and go after whatever sparks your imagination. Be curious, playful, and cocky. Get into some mischief. You might get caught or reprimanded for your tricks and pranks, but you're so charming that the punishment will be tempered with laughter and allowances for your youth or youthful behavior. You're full of life. Burn bright and let your energy bring joy to yourself and others.

This can be a time of freedom and exploration; take it. Learn everything you can, figure a few things out. Be a kid. The responsibilities of life will soon catch up with you, and you'll have to be an adult again, but today is not that day.

IF THIS IS SOMEONE ELSE IN YOUR LIFE

This is a child or someone who wants to be one. They're a creative and engaging presence, someone who can bring adventure and fun into your life if you let them. They're not equipped to take on big responsibilities, and they don't have a lot of experience in the world. They may get you into trouble, but you'll have fun along the way.

ACTIVATION

A little mischief is good for my soul.

♦ ♦ ♦

SPIRIT OF WANDS

You stir things up. You're a whirlwind and a thunderstorm on a hot night. You ride in, turn everything upside down, break hearts, and inspire people to heights of passion and fury, and then you ride back out again. You can't help it; you're on fire. You're the spark that incites change and unrest just by bringing your own fervor into any space.

Be bold and courageous. Chase after your ambitions, allowing the fire in your veins to spur you on. The long-term future isn't on your mind right now, and you're better off focusing on and completing one goal at a time before moving on to the next. Harness your fiery temperament into something productive rather than burning out.

IF THIS IS SOMEONE ELSE IN YOUR LIFE

This person can be the most fun you've had in a long time. Their energy is attractive and they're charismatic, but don't expect them to settle down or stay in one place for very long. Unless you're both on the same page, they can bring frustration or hurt feelings. This may be a brilliant but impatient person with a hot temper. Tread carefully.

ACTIVATION

I'm a free spirit.

◆ ◆ ◆

HEART OF WANDS

Your fire burns too bright for some. Your intense gaze unsettles others. That's okay. You didn't come into this life to make other people feel comfortable. You're just doing your own thing. Be unique. Be fierce, kind, and funny. Take up space without apology. Luxuriate in your own presence. Do what lights you up and makes you feel alive. Don't settle for lukewarm. While some people will shy away from you, others will be drawn like moths to a flame. You have a unique magic, genuine and confident, and you make people feel special when you decide to turn your attention to them.

Your intuition is always bang on, and your creativity crackles around you like wildfire. Give your intuition and creativity an outlet for expression—give them form. When you focus on what you're passionate about, the results astonish.

IF THIS IS SOMEONE ELSE IN YOUR LIFE

Fall under the spell of this person without losing yourself. Let them inspire you to be more truly yourself, rather than trying to emulate them. They're happy to help you, and to share their wisdom with you, and to cheer you on, but only up to a point. They're generous but impatient, preferring a kind of support that inspires self-sufficiency over hand-holding.

ACTIVATION

I'm a passionate creator.

◆ ◆ ◆

MIND OF WANDS

You're the visionary, innovator, and strategist. You can see the end goal, the prize that no one else could imagine, and then create a plan that will take you there. This is no small thing, to be a dreamer who also acts. You've learned from experience that dreams are nothing without follow-through. Although you're restless and driven, you have the maturity to manage and make good use of your energy. So, don't hesitate—pursue your ambitions with unshakable confidence, while armed with a flexible plan.

You're a natural leader, but this isn't always easy for you. You would rather explore, hunt, and conquer instead of directing others to do those things. Still, you take your role and responsibilities seriously. Your challenge is to rule without impatience or arrogance, to guide without being daunting or overbearing, and to sit still long enough to share your wisdom with those who seek it.

IF THIS IS SOMEONE IN YOUR LIFE

This person would be an excellent mentor. This is someone who can inspire you to go after your goals in life with confidence, and in your own unique way. They're fearless and will push you, but they're also protective and won't let you go too far. They won't be an equal partner; instead they will always take the lead and expect you to follow.

ACTIVATION

I have the heart of a lion.

CUPS

ACE OF CUPS

The universe is offering you a gift of love. You don't have to prove yourself worthy or go on a quest to find it; all you need to do is open your heart and receive it.

The Ace of Cups brings the promise of love and healing. To start this process, simply let your emotions flow, and cultivate compassion toward all beings, including yourself. The time is right to invite in a new love, or to embark on a creative project that's dear to your heart. With the Ace of Cups, possibilities are opening up. Let your emotions guide you to whatever fills your cup in the current moment.

ACTIVATION

I'm guided by love.

TWO OF CUPS

When you first meet someone whom your soul recognizes, it's magic. You reach out to each other, knowing that this moment is going to change your lives. The Two of Cups represents a significant meeting, one that's blessed, meant to be.

If you're seeking love or have made a new connection with someone, there's potential for something special here: an equal partnership, two hearts in alignment, a harmonious combination of opposites. If you're in a committed relationship, remember what brought you together in the first place. Be gentle with each other, recapture that miracle. If your loved one has passed on to the next plane of existence, know that their love is still around and a part of you. Many soulmates will cross your path in each lifetime, partners in love, friendship, and business, and each one will have something valuable to teach you.

ACTIVATION

I invite the magic of real connection into my life.

THREE OF CUPS

Friends who are with you through both the celebrations and tribulations of life are pure gold. They love you at your best, and at your worst, and in their company you never have to pretend to be someone that you aren't. When you need support, turn to your circle of friends. When your support is needed, give it. And above all, celebrate together. Celebrate the milestone occasions as well as the everyday moments. Fill your glasses and drink deeply of each other's company. The bond you share makes life sweeter and creates something beautiful that's greater than the sum total of your individual parts.

All friends are precious, but there's a special place for old friends. They really know you, your past and present self, and are ready to love your future self. See yourself through their eyes from time to time and appreciate how you've changed and grown throughout the years.

ACTIVATION

I cherish my friends.

FOUR OF CUPS

Things that you once enjoyed no longer satisfy and some pleasures have turned stale. This often happens gradually over time. You may not have as much in common with others as you used to, and you aren't sure what you want—but it isn't this ...

The dissatisfaction and resistance that you're feeling are evolutionary growing pains. Your priorities are changing, and you're in the process of understanding what will bring you greater satisfaction going forward. During this time, you may need to withdraw and meditate on what your heart is telling you. While this is time well spent, don't withdraw so deeply that you lose sight of the blessings that the universe is offering you. Have the presence of mind to reject what no longer makes you happy, while remaining open to new and unexpected sources of love and fulfillment.

ACTIVATION

I accept that growth and change are beneficial.

FIVE OF CUPS

Grief can feel like a raging river that engulfs you. On some level, you want it to engulf you and sweep you away; otherwise you'll have to adapt to and accept your new reality. Remember and grieve for what's lost. Do this consciously, and at your own pace. Your sadness and disappointment are the veil through which you're viewing the world right now, and it will take time to make sense of this altered perspective. And when you're ready, lift the veil and have a look at the blessings, love, and sources of joy that are still there for you. Because they're there, waiting for you to see them. Things have turned out differently than you'd hoped or planned for, but life will become brighter again if you can forgive yourself and the universe for how things played out.

ACTIVATION

I acknowledge what I've lost, and appreciate all that remains.

SIX OF CUPS

Immerse yourself in sweetness. You've had a strong dose of reality recently, and your heart longs for simpler and less complicated times. Your happy place calls, and there's nothing wrong with retreating to where all things are warm and fuzzy. Indulge yourself.

What makes you feel safe, loved, and playful? Perhaps happy memories that have become your own fairy tales. What or whom did you love when you were a child? Friends? Pets? Precious toys? The scent of roses or the ease of a summer day? When you need a break from the world, allow yourself a temporary escape to an idealized past that gives you insight and inspiration for happiness in your future. Remember that you also have the support of loved ones and happy moments to enjoy in the here and now.

ACTIVATION

I focus on what makes me happy.

SEVEN OF CUPS

It's good to have options. You have many in front of you right now, and at first glance they all look shiny and appealing. It's pleasant to lose yourself imagining how one choice might have an impact on your life, and how different the outcome would be with another. You could enjoy floating here for ages, because here, in this limbo, you don't have to limit yourself to one option or the risk of making the wrong choice. Everything remains possible.

Your imagination is a powerful ally. It can inform you and open up possibilities, so let it play for a while, but know that you're going to have to decide at some point. Otherwise, nothing will happen, and you'll stay right where you are. When you're ready to choose, be aware of how your emotions are coloring how you're seeing your options. Is your vision clear, or are you clouded? Step back, examine each option carefully, and make the best choice.

ACTIVATION

I make wise choices.

EIGHT OF CUPS

Your heart is restless and urges you to move beyond the comfortable and known. This may mean turning your back on someone or something that you still hold dear. Don't fear this path. Know that answering the call of your passion or acknowledging that it's time to let go of something that isn't working for you anymore isn't the same as running away. Follow the promptings of your soul and move forward.

You may decide to go on a physical journey, traveling to a place that's calling to you. Or your journey might be spiritual, leading to a place that's deep within you. You can't know how it will turn out, or plot a course that avoids risk and challenge, but you can go into the unknown with the conviction that the quest itself will be worth the effort. The first few steps are often the most difficult, but know that a new world is about to open up to you.

ACTIVATION

I have the courage to go wherever my heart leads.

NINE OF CUPS

Life is good. Gratitude fills your heart, and you wear your blessings and achievements like a crown for all the world to see. It's good to feel happy, and proud of yourself and all that you've accomplished. Your wishes have come true because of your steadfast heart, unwavering faith, and willingness to work toward your goals. Enjoy your good fortune wholeheartedly and share your optimism and happiness with those around you.

Count your blessings. When you focus on the people and circumstances that bring you joy, more will follow. You will never run out of opportunities for bliss, and there's no limit to the number of wishes that can come true for you. Enjoy this satisfaction, knowing that there's still room for further growth and even deeper expressions of love and compassion.

ACTIVATION

I'm grateful for all of my blessings.

TEN OF CUPS

You've reached your happily-ever-after place. And even better, you're surrounded by loved ones, with whom you can share it all. Joy is best when shared. The family members or kindred spirits with whom you're spending your life journey only enrich your experience and expand your capacity to love. They don't have to be perfect, and you don't have to be perfect, and everyday doesn't have to be an over-the-rainbow kind of day, but the love you have for each other allows for human foibles and twists of fate.

This is a time of harmony and contentment for you, so pause and savor it. Ask yourself how you can support your loved ones. What kindnesses can you offer? Your own happiness will multiply with every act of generosity and appreciation.

ACTIVATION

I'm part of a circle of universal love.

SOUL OF CUPS

You have the gift of delight. You're delighted by the world around you and are constantly surprised by the beauty and variety of life. You're a gentle dreamer who receives messages and signs from the universe with ease and can imagine possibilities far beyond anything you've seen or experienced. It's wonderful to see the world through the eyes of a child, without judgment and without analyzing the magic away.

Your sensitivity can leave your heart vulnerable and easily hurt. Nevertheless, stay curious and open to possibility. Creative inspiration arrives from unexpected sources. The Soul of Cups tells you to allow your inner child to come out and play. Make fun your goal. If you take this approach, your productivity will flow like a river, and all you'll have to do is float along with it.

IF THIS IS SOMEONE IN YOUR LIFE

Someone around you is seeking your approval. They want to be loved, although they may not be feeling entirely worthy. This could be a child, or someone who is childlike, so be patient with this individual. Don't expect them to be logical or rational, because they're expressing purely from the heart. Let them know that it's safe to express emotions; this will be healing for you as well.

ACTIVATION

*I find something that delights
me every day.*

◆ ◆ ◆

SPIRIT OF CUPS

You're love's sweet dream. Daring and bold, chivalrous, and beautiful. You're so romantic, so in love with love, that you unintentionally break hearts—and don't even notice. You see yourself as the hero, the star-crossed lover, and you're not wrong. There's nothing you won't do if it serves the cause of romantic love.

Be idealistic and dreamy, by all means, but don't get so lost in fantastical standards that no one, including yourself, can live up to. Stay in tune with the true vibration of love, letting your ideals elevate you and bring out your best.

We all have plenty of practical tasks that we need to manage, and mundane matters that need our attention, but just for now, put them aside and have an adventure. The Spirit of Cups asks you to follow your heart. If you so choose, your life can have fairy-tale elements such as honor and the realization of impossible dreams. Your heart's desire, whatever or whoever, awaits.

IF THIS IS SOMEONE IN YOUR LIFE

A Knight in Shining Armor comes riding into your life, offering you love or the opportunity to attain something that has great meaning for you. This paramour is romantic and seemingly earnest in the heat of the moment but has a changeable heart. Motivated by the quest and pursuit of love, once your heart's been achieved, they may stay or continue to go on to the next adventure. Break their heart, and you'll never be fully forgiven. Know that this person will always make decisions from the heart, which can be beautiful or devastating, depending on where they are in their life at this time.

ACTIVATION

I'm a hopeful romantic.

• • •

HEART OF CUPS

You make your home in an ocean of emotion. You enjoy floating in the shallows, but you also love going into the dark depths, where you're immersed in your feelings and visions. You believe that it's better to feel everything, rather than trying to hold back a tidal wave of emotion. It's tempting to get swept away, because your heart is your touchstone; still, you'll always know when it's time to bob to the surface.

Your intuition feeds your soul. You can see the past, present, and future, and you understand how they all interconnect. You know yourself well, and you see into the hearts of others with ease.

Your compassion is as vast as the ocean. Your first impulse is to heal those who are in pain, because you're able to feel and take on their pain as your own. You need to learn how to observe the emotions of others without drowning in them, to heal without depleting yourself. Keep your own cup filled, and keep it close.

IF THIS IS SOMEONE IN YOUR LIFE

This person cares for you and wants the best for you. They will listen, offering good advice, comfort, and a shoulder to cry on while resisting the urge to fix everything. If you're in a close relationship with this person, regardless if it's a lover, friend, or family member, they will want all of you. They're comfortable in their own emotions, so don't be surprised if this Heart will want access to all of your thoughts and feelings as well. At this relationship's most challenging, these Hearts may hold on too tightly or demand an intensity of connection that's difficult to satisfy.

ACTIVATION

I'm at home with my emotions.

◆ ◆ ◆

MIND OF CUPS

You're wise and unshakable. You've learned that everything happens in its own time, and your understanding of human nature is boundless. In times of sadness and doubt, you carry those who're sinking. You take your responsibilities seriously and carry the world on your back. Although you assume the role of supporter and advisor for those in your care, you resist having to fix or figure out everything for them. You provide a haven in the storm, but what they do after that is up to them.

You've been hurt before and have learned some tough life lessons, but you've healed and developed a shell that protects the parts of you that are soft and vulnerable. You're generous and kind, and your emotions always factor into your plans, goals, and strategies, but you aren't ruled by them. You don't get swallowed by waves of emotion. Instead, they part like the seas to let you pass through now, while propelling you forward. You're the one in charge of your own heart and mind.

IF THIS IS SOMEONE IN YOUR LIFE

You can tell this person anything. Go to this Mind when you can't keep your head above water. They will listen without judgment, advise you well, and then keep your situation confidential. While you can rely on this Mind to be kind, don't expect to be completely indulged. Their wisdom might come from the heart, but useful action, steps, and strategy will also be offered. If you're in a relationship with this Mind of Cups, know that although they love you with a great depth of feeling, it might not be as openly expressed.

ACTIVATION

I have rulership over my emotions.

SWORDS

ACE OF SWORDS

The Ace of Swords is a eureka moment. Something that has been puzzling you becomes crystal clear. In a flash of insight, the truth comes to light, and you discover a new way of thinking. You can see the way forward.

However, this way forward arrives with a challenge. If you have the courage to act in alignment with your higher purpose, to speak your truth and fight for what you believe in, you'll achieve success. Personal victory depends on conviction in yourself, and a willingness to be honest and clear, even when it stings. Will you pick up the sword?

ACTIVATION

I'm thinking in a new way.

TWO OF SWORDS

You're at the crossroads, facing an important decision. It's taking a lot of energy to remain where you are, but you're not budging. It's better to hold your ground until you've gathered all the relevant information and processed everything spinning through your mind. Although it may be best to rely on your logical side, also let your intuition inform this situation. If your heart and mind are fighting each other, it will make the decision more difficult, so encourage them to work together instead.

While you're thinking things through, uphold personal boundaries. The careless or hurtful words of others could throw you off balance, so protect your heart and tune out negative distractions or pressures that force you into making a choice before you're ready.

ACTIVATION

I make balanced decisions.

THREE OF SWORDS

You've experienced pain in the past that still feels like swords piercing your heart. You thought that surely your heart must have broken; yet, despite the hurt and betrayal, you've discovered that it still beats strongly.

Nevertheless, these are deep wounds. You still need time to heal, and to process these painful memories. While there may not be the option of resolution or restitution, deep reflection on your grief, anger, or unhappiness can provide new wisdom and perspective that you need to begin the healing and acceptance process. What's done is done. Now you have the power to manage your thoughts and choose how you want to see yourself. This has been a difficult and undesirable life lesson, but you don't need to carry the pain forever. Your heart will be whole again.

ACTIVATION

I value even the hardest of life's lessons.

FOUR OF SWORDS

It's time to rest. You've had a lot on your mind recently, and you've fought your share of battles, but for now, put down your swords and withdraw. The stress that you've been under has taken its toll on your body, mind, and spirit. The best care that you can give yourself in this moment is stillness, quiet, and rest. Retreat from the world and make achieving greater peace of mind your priority. Healing will follow.

Your best practice at this time includes meditation, prayer, and mindfulness, or anything that helps you quiet your thoughts. And when you sleep, make this a sacred time, inviting in sweet dreams or allowing yourself to sink into comforting nothingness. You'll be more equipped for any battles that lie ahead if you take this time to replenish yourself.

ACTIVATION

I allow myself to rest and heal.

FIVE OF SWORDS

Tensions are high. There's a vibration of anger around you. While it doesn't belong to you, take care that it's not directed at you. The current atmosphere is charged with fear and fury, making constructive communication impossible. It's better to walk away than try to confront the chaos or an energy that's impervious to reason.

If you're under attack, your reaction may be either to try to solve and soothe the situation or to fight back. If you choose either of those options, it's likely that you'll end up getting bitten, or you might become the growling dog. With all the noise and angry words, you can't hear yourself think, nor can the other party hear your rational words over their own snarls, resulting in futile communication. The wisest course of action in this moment is to retreat, even if it means cutting your losses.

ACTIVATION

I know when to walk away.

SIX OF SWORDS

You've come through tough and trying times and can finally see the other side. You're carrying the weight of your experiences and memories with you on this journey, but what will help unpack the burden is the knowledge that slowly but surely, you're sailing toward brighter days. It may feel strange right now to be surrounded by peace and quiet after so much stress. It might be difficult to simply let things unfold, but during this time of transition, don't fight the current, and keep your focus on moving forward.

ACTIVATION

I'm ready to move on.

SEVEN OF SWORDS

You're good at getting in and out of tricky situations and can boast your share of shenanigans. If you're thinking of taking a gamble, the Seven of Swords suggests that you'll come up with ingenious schemes that no one else could have imagined or would dare do. This kind of resourcefulness is what you need to call upon right now.

You have an opportunity for personal gain, but there's also risk involved. If you decide to pursue what you desire, you'll need to be clever and as quick as a fox. Look for ways to shift the situation to your own benefit without disclosing your motivations or methods. Keep your eyes open and analyze what people are saying to you, rather than accepting everything at face value. Roll the dice with humor and style, and if you get pinched, meet the consequences with goodwill.

ACTIVATION

I understand what's at stake.

EIGHT OF SWORDS

If you allow self-critical and negative thoughts to run unchecked, before you know it you'll feel completely surrounded by them and caged. All those harsh things that you say to and about yourself, then ruminate over, will eventually turn you to stone and make it difficult to assess your options and resources.

Listen to and question the ongoing stories that you tell yourself. Are they accurate? Necessary? Supportive? Have you made yourself the villain of your own story? If so, adjust your perspective. You always have choices. You're not powerless. There's a way out of this trap, and since you're the one who has built this cage, you can also find your way out.

ACTIVATION

I'm not powerless.

NINE OF SWORDS

Thoughts and memories keep you awake at night. They're flying around your mind, pecking and cawing, disturbing your sleep. In this surreal place of fatigue fueled by adrenaline, perspective flies out the window. Worries become larger than life, and vague fears overshadow the reality of your situation.

Stop torturing yourself and take a breath. You can't change the past, and you can't control the future. Right now, you're okay. It's difficult to see things clearly when you're in a cloud of regret about what's happened, and anxious about what might happen. Bring those thoughts into the light and take away their power. You may want to talk to someone. Everyone experiences dark thoughts and shadows; you're not alone.

ACTIVATION

I ask for help when I need it.

TEN OF SWORDS

Exhale. It's done. You can't sustain this level of stress or suffering any longer. You have nothing left to give, and there's no point sacrificing yourself any longer. Whatever has felt like a thousand cuts has played out. You may not be ready, but nevertheless it ends now.

Whether you've been betrayed or feel you've let yourself down, the Ten of Swords says let it die. Take solace in the fact that you've already been through the worst of it, and there's nowhere to go but up. And once it's all over, you'll feel not only a release but a sense of relief. Surrendering will make space for a new beginning that will be transformational. The sun will rise tomorrow, and you'll be there to greet it.

ACTIVATION

I'm ready to transform.

SOUL OF SWORDS

You're a breath of fresh air that's hard to ignore. You're sharp and love to ask questions that go straight to the heart of the matter, and you don't give up until you get your answer. You have an insatiable curiosity and seek a constant stream of information to categorize and pin down. Always ready to take on something new, even when you have no experience or knowledge, you're prepared to give it your best shot.

Your keen eye never misses a thing. While you take great pleasure in sharing your observations, you haven't yet learned when keeping your thoughts and rash comments to yourself is better than speaking a hurtful truth. With such a sharp intellect, you may be driven to want to know it all. Enjoy this time of discovery and learning without feeling like you have to be right, or the need to always prove your point.

IF THIS IS SOMEONE IN YOUR LIFE

This Soul wants to prove themselves and is determined to get things right, even without fully formed skills or experience. Before taking on this Soul of Swords, keep in mind that you'll experience more success with a committed course of instruction and guidance. Know you'll have a quick learner without any guile. While you'll always get brutally honest feedback, answers, or opinions, beware the impact: they don't have the empathy to sugarcoat their communication.

ACTIVATION

I don't have to know it all at once.
I learn along the way.

♦ ♦ ♦

SPIRIT OF SWORDS

You don't do things by half. You fly through life full throttle, a swift hunter who never loses sight of their prey. You have an innate sense of timing, and you understand the importance of acting at the right moment. There's always a prize to be won, a cause to be championed, or someone in distress who needs to be rescued, and you rise to the challenge, every time.

Your single-mindedness is powerful. It drives you toward your goals and feeds your ambition. When you're fixated on a particular target, everything else fades into the periphery. Anything you set your mind on, you achieve. Even if gentler pleasures and slower companions get left behind.

Stillness is difficult for you, but if you don't slow down on occasion, at least, you're going to rush through your life, right past opportunities for love, discovery, connection, and comfort.

IF THIS IS SOMEONE IN YOUR LIFE

Give this Spirit a task or ask for their help, and you won't be let down. However, you'll experience a level of focus and intensity that can be overwhelming. If this Spirit of Sword's eye is fixed on you, you'll feel like the center of the universe. But should this focus stray, and it does, it's futile to get back the attention. Don't take it personally or else you'll have to suffer the hurt feelings that inevitably come when dealing with a brash Spirit of Swords.

ACTIVATION

I know where to focus my energy.

♦ ♦ ♦

HEART OF SWORDS

You're formidable. You see right through people and know instantly whom you're dealing with after hearing only a few words. You've seen and heard it all—and you don't have the time or patience for excuses, or tiptoeing around the facts or truth. Your words always hit their mark. You have a knack for finding people's softest spots, then saying exactly what needs to be said. People are willing to risk your sharp words because your advice is always right on point.

You are ruled by your head, but your judgment is tempered by your heart. The pain that you've personally experienced has made you wise, and as strong as steel. You haven't forgotten what it is to love, make mistakes, and suffer loss. You've learned many tough lessons, which has forged an ironclad conviction in yourself. While you're perfectly capable of making decisions that are unwavering and unapologetic, you still retain empathy for others; yet, the truth of any situation, as you see it, will always take precedence.

In your pursuit of truth, don't become unforgiving or overly critical. Don't be too quick to cut others out of your life when they don't uphold your high expectations. You're self-reliant, but that doesn't mean that you need to be alone on a lofty perch.

IF THIS IS SOMEONE IN YOUR LIFE

There's no point sugarcoating or stretching the truth with this Heart of Swords—cut straight to the chase. Coddling is not in this Heart's nature. Tough love can sting, but it's better to shake off the shock to your ego, then listen carefully to advice that will help you in leaps and bounds. This Heart will have no problem telling you to pull yourself together, and to get out there and just do what needs to be done. If you're willing to have a rational and honest discussion, this is an invaluable source for clarity, new perspectives, or conflict management and resolution.

ACTIVATION

I speak my truth.

• • •

MIND OF SWORDS

You're cool and collected. You always know what to say, and you say it perfectly. Your observation skills are unnerving, and you understand people's fears and motivations so precisely. Are you psychic? You insist that it's just your logical brain that loves a good puzzle. You value truth and facts above all, but you're still flexible enough to look at things from every angle and adjust your conclusions on the basis of your findings.

You enjoy keeping boundaries and distance, preferring to look at the world from a higher vantage point rather than getting tangled up in the complexities of human emotion. You soar high so that you can see the bigger plan, while ensuring that everything is running according to your strategy.

You're a wise advisor with a long memory—and crystal-clear vision. You record everything you see and retain an information bank to draw on when you need to formulate a decision. In your fascination with facts and figures and the true nature of existence, don't divorce yourself from what it's like to be fallible. There's always information to be gained from the messier, more confused or imperfect aspects of life.

IF THIS IS SOMEONE IN YOUR LIFE

You can trust this Mind of Swords. Do you need help seeing the reality of a situation? Or sage guidance that leads to a problem solved? Or maybe you have a goal without a sound strategy? If so, the Mind of Swords is a reliable resource. You'll receive the benefit of extensive knowledge that will be shared without reservation; just don't expect a pep talk or a sympathetic ear.

ACTIVATION

I'm discerning with my thoughts and words.

PENTACLES

ACE OF PENTACLES

You have a bright, shiny gold coin in your hand. Feel the weight of it. You've been gifted a valuable resource that's ready to be nurtured and used. It could be something tangible, such as a new job or business venture, a payment or windfall, or a new home, but more than likely it's YOU.

The Ace of Pentacles could also be saying that this is a good time to make an investment in your shiny, precious self. It encourages you to take a new approach to your overall well-being, since the changes you make now will come to fruition in time. Plant seeds now for your future financial security, health, and contentment.

ACTIVATION

I'm my own greatest resource.

TWO OF PENTACLES

You're walking a tightrope right now, gracefully navigating the ups and downs of life's competing demands. It takes a lot of concentration to maintain balance. It feels great when you get into your groove, but constantly being on the edge doesn't leave you any space to think, rest, or plan for the future.

What are you juggling? Your finances? Work/life balance? Your various roles and responsibilities? Explore how you can adjust and streamline your routine so that life flows more smoothly. Even though you're handling things well, the Two of Pentacles suggests that you may want to release some pressure by focusing on your highest priorities, then simplifying the rest. If you can get your practical matters in order, they'll start to run on their own momentum, freeing up your energy for bigger things.

ACTIVATION

I'm flexible and adaptable.

THREE OF PENTACLES

A beautiful buzz is created when a team works well together. Every team member brings their own unique skills and talents, creativity and productivity increase, and there's the satisfaction of working toward a shared goal.

You're capable and independent, but you're involved in a situation where collaboration is favored. Being a good team player brings sweeter results and opens greater possibilities. By leading, bringing a team together, or playing an individual role, you'll be able to achieve more than you would on your own. Whether this affects your career or community, the Three of Pentacles reminds you that cooperation is key: you're creating important relationships and mutual appreciation that will continue to bloom long after your involvement at this time.

ACTIVATION

I enjoy being part of a good team.

FOUR OF PENTACLES

You have money on your mind. Finances are solid, yet you're ruminating on how much you have and wondering if it's enough. Having money in the bank gives you a feeling of safety. It's also a source of constant worry. If you insist that money equals peace of mind, you may not see other sources of support and satisfaction, while distancing youself from your spiritual side.

The Four of Pentacles invites you to examine your relationship with money. Is it a positive force, or does it bring up feelings of insecurity and fear? Are you blocking your own flow because you're clutching material things too tightly? If a scarcity mindset prevents you from enjoying your life fully, adopt an attitude that fosters more appreciation for the resources that you have. Embrace the idea that there's enough to go around for everyone. Be mindful of your money but manage it without letting it dominate your perspective.

ACTIVATION

I invite the flow of prosperity.

FIVE OF PENTACLES

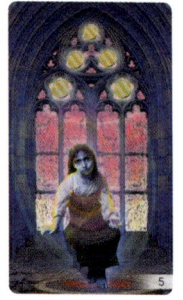

Are you feeling like a ghost floating around in your own life? Are you moving through the world unseen, suffering hardships and loss, disconnected from others who aren't understanding your experience?

During these shadowy tests of faith, remember to look up. There's help available to you. You don't have to stay out in the cold. Help comes in many forms. The Five of Pentacles assures you that there's a warm, welcoming place waiting for you. Seek assistance. During a time of spiritual crisis, call upon your Spirit Guides; consult your Higher Self or your loved ones in Spirit. If your world has become unstable due to financial challenges, look to community support, helping institutions, and experienced professionals who can help you navigate these hardships.

ACTIVATION

I reach out for help when I need it.

SIX OF PENTACLES

The universe runs on a flow of giving and receiving. If you're in a position to share your resources, whether that's money, time, or energy, give openhandedly. If you could benefit from some help, receive it just as freely and fully.

Give and take is a simple and natural process. How do you feel when someone offers you a gift, a compliment, or financial support? Does it make you feel uncomfortable? If so, you're not alone. How does it feel when you're the one giving the gift? Are you always the one giving? Does this make you feel more comfortable? Challenge yourself to give without expectations, and to receive without questioning. As human beings, we rely on each other; we're all connected, and one of the most beautiful ways to experience that connection is through the simple act of offering or accepting a gift.

ACTIVATION

I give and receive joyfully.

SEVEN OF PENTACLES

You've persevered in the face of challenge, adapted through feast and famine, and now you're starting to see the tangible results of your efforts. Growth has been slow but steady, and you can be proud of what you've achieved so far. There's more work ahead, but before you head back into the thick of it, pause and step back.

The Seven of Pentacles offers you an opportunity to examine the progression of your work or a goal. When you revisit the bigger purpose, do you find that you're still acting in alignment, or is some adjustment necessary? Are you maintaining a balanced life and nurturing all aspects of it? Are you still finding joy and satisfaction in what you're doing? Although you're eager to keep going and finish what you've set out to do, don't miss this Seven of Pentacles chance to reflect or realign.

ACTIVATION

I know when to recalibrate my energy and intention.

EIGHT OF PENTACLES

You're busy as a bee, and so productive. Now's a good time to keep your head down, immerse yourself in your work or project, and get things done. Be present in the moment and fully focused on what you're doing. Let the world become a pleasant din in the background as you focus on what's right in front of you. Won't it be satisfying to complete all those tasks that have been piling up?

The Eight of Pentacles reminds you to enjoy the process rather than lusting after the outcome. You're on a path toward prosperity, one that's paved by consistent effort and repetition. Keep it up and you'll soon discover that your skill and expertise increase exponentially.

ACTIVATION

I gain satisfaction from my work.

NINE OF PENTACLES

You've worked hard to create your best life, so inhale as much of its sweetness as you can. You know yourself well, and you know what it's taken to get to this place of ease and abundance. You have the confidence and discipline to know when to work and strive, and when to relax.

Thanks to your consistent efforts, your practical and financial matters are in good order. You're free to enjoy the sanctuary of your own company within an environment that brings you pleasure. Go ahead and surround yourself with beautiful things. Love your life.

ACTIVATION

I enjoy a rich and abundant life.

TEN OF PENTACLES

You've put down deep roots into fertile soil, and everything is growing. By committing yourself to longer-term goals rather than short-term gain, you've created a life of abundance and security for yourself and your loved ones. This prosperity will last.

The Ten of Pentacles signals worldly success and financial stability, but it goes deeper. It represents your family tree, your ancestral lineage, and your place within. You're part of the expanding network of time with roots in the past, and the future extends through and beyond you. Your ancestors are a source of wisdom and support. Reach out to them whenever you need guidance. Remember that you too will become an ancestor, so be mindful about the legacy beyond material success that you're creating in this lifetime.

ACTIVATION

I'm creating my legacy.

SOUL OF PENTACLES

You're a child of forests and fields with a deep reverence for all living things. Nature delights you, and you're happiest outside under an open sky with your fingers and toes connecting with the earth. You're a protector of small creatures, and a nurturer of everything that grows.

Your learning style is hands on, and you love to see the tangible results of your efforts. You're often serious, and people think you're shy, but you prefer to consider your words rather than using them carelessly. Sometimes the enormity of the world overwhelms you. You feel vulnerable and small, and afraid of making mistakes or losing something that's valuable to you.

Whenever you venture out of your garden or your comfort zone, you proceed slowly and cautiously. You like to do your best and take small steps rather than racing ahead. You have a lot to discover, and you'll learn and grow as you go. You can feel optimistic about what will flourish in good time.

IF THIS IS SOMEONE IN YOUR LIFE

Be gentle with this Soul of Pentacles, who startles easily and may run away. You'll find this Soul the happiest in their own world, fascinated by the moment and whatever it has to offer, so there's no use getting frustrated when this Soul is slow to answer or act. This Soul of Pentacles has lots of potential and wants to work and study hard and do very well, but you'll need to push and prod if you want to create an equally powerful distraction.

ACTIVATION

I take my own time to learn, grow, and flourish.

❖ ❖ ❖

SPIRIT OF PENTACLES

You're the rock that everyone relies on. You're the quiet protector, the patient companion. Your back is strong, and so you shoulder other people's problems as if they're your own, no questions asked and no solutions offered. You're comfortable in your strength. You know your capabilities and how to handle yourself. You never need to put on a big show to prove anything.

Slow and steady is your mantra. You like to be prepared, have a plan, and stick to it. You're not good with last-minute changes, and you get annoyed if someone tries to rush you into doing a sloppy job. You would rather take your time and get it right the first time.

You are conscientious and diligent, so much so that life can become painstaking, an ongoing exercise in patience. Recognize when you're being stubborn instead of determined, and get used to the fact that life sometimes throw curves for which you can't always prepare in advance. Thankfully, you have that strong protective armor.

IF THIS IS SOMEONE IN YOUR LIFE

The Spirit of Pentacles can easily carry you when you're tired and need support. They may not understand what you're going through or be able to say what you want to hear, but they won't leave your side until you let it be known that you're ready. This Spirit will wait for you to ask for help, without pushing or presuming, and will be more than happy and willing. You may wish that the Spirit of Pentacles was more forthcoming or moved a little bit faster, but it's not going to happen, so don't take it to heart.

ACTIVATION

I go at my own pace.

♦ ♦ ♦

HEART OF PENTACLES

You're the Earth Mother. You instinctively know what people need to grow and flourish, and you provide it generously. You're the one whom everyone runs to when they have a scraped knee, a broken heart, or financial woes. You know how to run a household or a business or a planet with efficiency and kindness, and money always rolls in. Practical solutions never elude you, people feel safe around you, and life seems manageable when you're around.

Nature and the physical world delight and sustain you. Of all the Pentacles folk, you, most of all, understand that our time on Earth is finite, and there's wisdom in the cycle of life, death, and rebirth. You use your time well and appreciate the pleasures that your five senses provide. Pragmatism is your default, but you never lose sight of the magic and miracles in all creation.

Independence is important to you. You take care of everyone else, but you also know that you can rely on yourself when it comes to your home, your finances, and the creation of a satisfying life. You can always find or manifest whatever you need.

IF THIS IS SOMEONE IN YOUR LIFE

Go to this Heart whenever you need solid advice and sensible solutions. You won't experience judgment or be told what should have been done differently. Expect instead an examination of your current situation, and assistance in getting it thoroughly sorted. After a good conversation and a hug, you'll feel better about yourself and your world, armed with a new sense of direction and restored by the exact healing that you needed.

ACTIVATION

I am powerful, practical, and kind.

♦ ♦ ♦

MIND OF PENTACLES

You know how to live well. You've built up your wealth, power, and expertise through bullheaded dedication to your goals, and now you can indulge in the many pleasures that this earth has to offer. Luxury surrounds you, good food and drink, the best of everything.

A master of finance and business, you recognize and seize every opportunity to increase your wealth and domain, while protecting what you already have. This doesn't mean that you're a miser; quite the opposite, in fact. You share your resources generously, whether this is money, time, energy, or guidance.

Not much can upset or surprise you, but when you're pushed too far, you dig in your heels and never concede to ultimatums. You're slow to anger, but when you get there, your rage is terrifying, but thankfully short lived.

IF THIS IS SOMEONE IN YOUR LIFE

The Mind of Pentacles can teach you a lot about the world. Ambitious, expect that this Mind has earned a powerful position through sustained effort and determination. When dealing with this dedicated individual, expect toughness and high expectations, but also know that you'll be generously given all the tools or resources that you'll need to attain your own success. If you're fiery or impatient, this Mind's signature stubbornness and leisurely pace could drive you to distraction.

ACTIVATION

I know how to live well.

❖ ❖ ❖

HOW TO READ TAROT

A great Tarot reading is a conversation between the Reader, the cards, and the Seeker, the person who's getting their cards read. Getting a reading is like sitting down with a trusted friend, someone who knows and loves you and will always tell the truth without judgment. The same holds true if you're reading for yourself.

When you read the cards, you're calling on your knowledge of the Tarot, your own life experience, and your intuition. But there's more. The images on the cards help you connect with the highest part of yourself or your Sitter with a collective source of wisdom, love, and memory.

There are many ways to read Tarot. You'll find your own style and voice. Reading the cards in the way that feels natural to you, rather than trying to emulate someone else, will light you up and fire your intuition. As you get to know the cards, and yourself as a Reader, enjoy the process. You don't have to be perfect or amaze anyone with your uncanny insight; just be yourself.

To get started, I invite you to create your own Tarot ritual. The purpose of creating a personal Tarot ritual is to allow you to shift into a sacred energetic space, where you feel confident and open to receiving the messages that the cards are sending you. In order to inspire you to create your own Tarot ritual, here are some of the elements that I include in my own process.

SETTING THE SCENE

Ground and center yourself and release any expectations that you have around the outcome of the reading. Take a few deep breaths while imagining that you're infusing your body with white light. The Violet Flame can also help with this. You can clear your cards and your space by using the same process, by sending white or violet light to them.

In my opinion, no other tools are necessary aside from you and the cards, but I love adding beautiful and shiny things to my ritual. I use a spread cloth on my table, and I lay out crystals and representations of the deity or guide whom I'm working with. For *The Unifying Consciousness Tarot* in particular, I use crystal carvings of the Platonic solids to call upon their elemental energies for support and guidance.

INVOCATION

Create an invocation that you recite, silently or out loud, before you start your reading. Again, this isn't required, but it's powerful. You're letting the universe, Source, your Guides, Spirit—however you define the force that you're connecting with—know your intention for the reading, and that you're open to receive it. An invocation is deeply personal, and it elevates the reading experience to something sacred.

Here's an invocation that I created for *The Unifying Consciousness Tarot*:

> *May this reading awaken us*
> *to our eternal nature, our*
> *interconnectedness, and raise us to the*
> *highest vibration of love.*
> *May the elements of air, fire, water, and*
> *earth support and guide us,*
> *and may Spirit inspire us. I am grateful*
> *for every moment of this life and for this*
> *opportunity to read the cards in this*
> *healing way.*

FORMING THE QUESTION

A good question is the basis of the reading. Ask a good question and you'll get a clear and powerful answer. Questions give you something to work with, an action you can take, a new perspective or confirmation, information that's more useful than a simple yes or no answer.

Craft empowering questions rather than fatalistic ones, so instead of "Will I ever …?" or "Will that other person ever …?," ask "How can I …?" or "What do I need to focus on to …?" The cards support you in reaching your goals and achieving your dreams when you acknowledge your own role and power in this equation.

CHOOSING A TAROT SPREAD

A Tarot spread is the pattern in which we lay out the cards. Each position in the spread is a mini question; it adds pieces of information to the main question that's being asked. Choose a spread, or create one, that fits your question, rather than trying to fit it into something that just doesn't work. I've included some example spreads that I've created for *The Unifying Consciousness Tarot* later in this chapter.

SHUFFLING THE CARDS

Keep your question in your mind as you shuffle the cards. I shuffle until it feels like it's enough, and then I cut the cards and deal off the top. Any kind of shuffling is fine as long as you can do it comfortably. By choosing a particular way of shuffling the cards, it becomes a part of your ritual, and you won't second-guess yourself when you lay out the cards. You'll know that they'll be just the right ones.

LAYING OUT AND READING THE CARDS

I lay out all of my cards in my Tarot spreads at the same time, face up. You may want to lay yours face down and reveal them one by one. Do whatever feels comfortable. Once all the cards are face up in front of you, have a look at them and allow a first intuitive blast of information to hit you before you start to break down the cards in their spread positions. Notice how the cards make you feel; notice any repeating suits, symbols, colors, patterns, or numbers;

and get the holistic lay of the land before your logical brain kicks in.

Now, go through the cards in their spread positions. You are looking to connect the message of the card to the position of the spread, and to the main question that you've asked. Pay attention to how the cards relate to each other as well. Are the figures on the cards looking at each other or turning away? Do you see movement in the same direction, or is there conflict? Notice how the cards exist in their positions. How are they playing with one another in the spread?

Take your time and absorb everything. Speak out loud, even if you're just reading for yourself. And when you're ready, circle back and take a look at the whole story again. What do you notice now? Be open to all messages, while ensuring that you've received an answer to your question. Don't worry if you don't completely understand it all at the time. Make notes or an entry in your journal and contemplate a bit further on the cards. Sometimes insights will come to you days after you originally did the reading.

CLOSING
THE READING

Once you feel that you've received everything that you can from the cards, close the reading. Do this just like your opening invocation, in a way that resonates with you. The main idea is that you're sending gratitude to your guides, or the universe, or Source for everything that you've experienced. Also send gratitude to the person you've read for, while saying farewell and releasing any energetic ties.

❖ ❖ ❖

TAROT SPREADS

THE BLUE ROSE SPREAD

Use this spread to connect with the energy of *The Unifying Consciousness Tarot* and to activate your spiritual awareness.

1. How can I resonate with the highest vibration of love?
2. How can I awaken to my eternal nature?
3. How can I connect with Source with greater ease?
4. What guide, guardian, or aspect of Source is around me now?
5. What message does this guide have for me?

THE UNIFYING CONSCIOUSNESS TAROT

ALL-SEEING EYE SPREAD

Use this spread when you're seeking guidance and perspective about a particular situation.

1. Tell me about this situation.
2. What's the best way to approach it?
3. What's the lesson here for me?
4. How can I transmute this situation for my highest good?
5. Is there anything I can do or need to do?
6. Is there anything I can't do or need to release?
7. How can I find an aspect of love in this situation?
8. A card to remind me of who I really am (can choose actively or randomly)

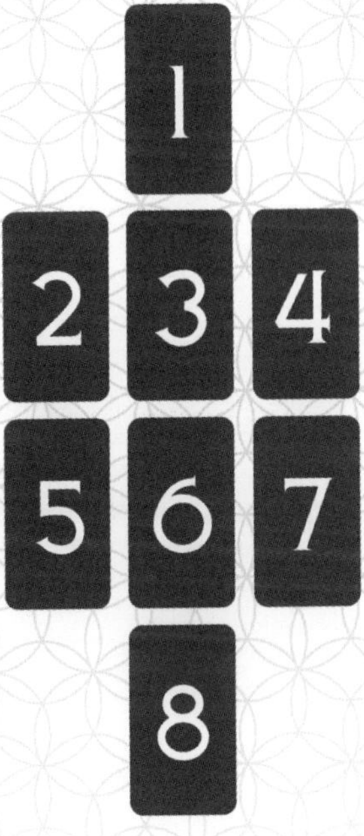
1
2
3
4
5
6
7
8

THE UNIFYING CONSCIOUSNESS TAROT

ACTIVATION SPREAD

Clearly define your goal or desire in your mind. As you shuffle, ask the cards for guidance on how you can fully activate your goal, bring it to life energetically, and start to manifest it in the world. Deal from the top of the deck and find the first Sword card, then continue until a Wand appears, a Cup, a Pentacle, and a Major Arcana card. Each of these cards offers advice that's coming specifically from their element and area of life. The card that follows the Major Arcana in the deck is the Activation. This is the action or attitude you can take to understand how you can fully use your gifts and capabilities to manifest your goal.

1. Swords/Air
2. Wands/Fire
3. Cups/Water
4. Pentacles/Earth
5. Major/Spirit or Aether
6. Activation

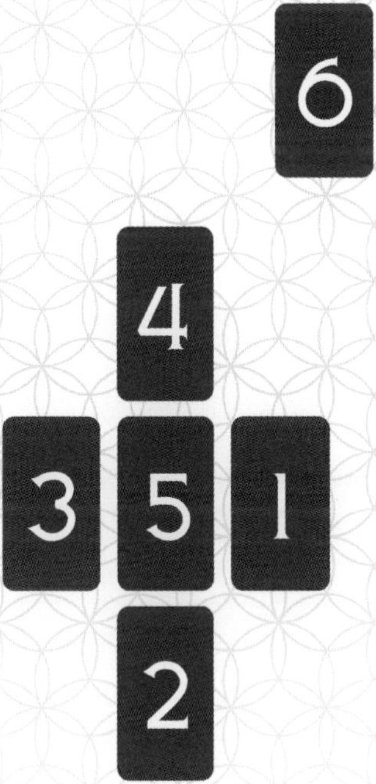
6
4
3
5
1
2

HEART-CENTERED ACTION SPREAD

Use this spread to help you to move toward living your purpose and achieving your goals in a heart-centered way.

1. How do I want to feel? (Choose this card actively. Select it face up from the deck. It's the card that most closely illustrates your desired feeling or state of being.)

   Now shuffle your deck and randomly select your next cards.

2. What will help me feel that way?
3. What could block that feeling?
4. What resources can I call upon in times of challenge?
5. What concrete action can I take to start moving toward that feeling?
6. An inspirational message from Source

May you be guided by the Unifying Consciousness of Love.

ABOUT THE CREATORS

photo credit: Matthew Brown

LORI LYTLE, a.k.a. Inner Goddess Tarot, is a lifelong Tarot reader and teacher who left office life to pursue a full-time career as a spiritual seeker and Tarot practitioner. Her approach to Tarot is both mystical and practical—she views the Tarot as a source of inspiration and a means of connection with the divine, as well as an everyday tool that can improve our lives in the here and now. Lori is an introvert, empath, nerd, solitary witch, High Priestess, Gemini, overthinker, and devotee of cats and cards. *The Unifying Consciousness Tarot* is Lori's first Tarot deck and book.

LEO SCOPACASA graduated from the Ontario College of Art with a focus on illustration and design and went on to provide editorial illustration for various publications in Canada, the US, and Japan. In 1997, Leo founded and established the Orbital Arts Gallery in Toronto as his studio and gallery to create and showcase art that awakens our understanding that we are all connected, and that universal spiritual love is our true nature. His inspiring artwork is found all over the world, and his gallery is a fixture in Toronto, beloved by artists and art lovers. Leo refers to his creations as Activation Art, designed to channel and allow users to access the energetic vibration of universal love that comes as a gift from his heart.

Find out more about the deck and its creators:
Lori Lytle
Inner Goddess Tarot
innergoddesstarot.com

Leo Scopacasa
Orbital Arts Gallery
orbitalarts.ca

Instagram @unifyingconsciousnesstarot

Copyright © 2025 by Lori Lytle, illustrations by Leo Scopacasa

Library of Congress Control Number: 2024941758

All rights reserved. No part of this work may be reproduced or used in any form or by any means—graphic, electronic, or mechanical, including photocopying or information storage and retrieval systems—without written permission from the publisher.

The scanning, uploading, and distribution of this book or any part thereof via the Internet or any other means without the permission of the publisher is illegal and punishable by law. Please purchase only authorized editions and do not participate in or encourage the electronic piracy of copyrighted materials.

"Red Feather Mind Body Spirit" logo is a trademark of Schiffer Publishing, Ltd.
"Red Feather Mind Body Spirit Feather" logo is a registered trademark of Schiffer Publishing, Ltd.

Designed by BMac
Cover design by BMac
Type set in Medusca/Copperplate/Acumin

ISBN: 978-0-7643-6912-4
Printed in China

Published by REDFeather Mind, Body, Spirit
An imprint of Schiffer Publishing, Ltd.
4880 Lower Valley Road
Atglen, PA 19310
Phone: (610) 593-1777; Fax: (610) 593-2002
Email: Info@redfeathermbs.com
Web: www.redfeathermbs.com